USA
Florida
and the Bahamas

Jarrold Publishing

CONTENTS

Introducing Florida   3
Essential details in brief   6
Life in Florida   7
Signposts of history   9
Food and drink – a guide for overseas visitors   10

Hints for your holiday: for overseas visitors   12
Where to go and what to see   13
The east coast   13
The west coast   38
Central Florida   49
The north-west   58

Introducing the Bahamas   61
Essential details in brief   63
Signposts of history   64
Food and drink   65

Where to go and what to see   67
New Providence – the capital island   67
Grand Bahama   74
The Family Islands   77

Useful things to know   89
Florida   89
The Bahamas   92

Index   95

Maps and plans
Florida   15, 21, 23, 56
Bahamas
          66, 68, 70, 76, 78, 80, 81, 83, 84, 85, 86, 87, 88
Reference map   back cover

Title page: Walt Disney World

Madeira Beach, Pinellas Suncoast

Introducing Florida

Where in the world would you go to spend a relatively inexpensive holiday in the sun at any time of the year, with nearly 1,500 miles of beaches on two coasts to choose from, be able to hire a car and visit different places of interest every day, and live in a superb holiday apartment? Florida, of course. Until only ten years ago the 'Sunshine State' was the preserve of the wealthy. The likes of Frank Sinatra may regret it, but the days are gone when only Hollywood stars and Wall Street bankers rubbed shoulders in the Miami Beach casinos. At first the American middle class began to flood in, and now a new wave of tourists has arrived from Europe.

In the last decade, good exchange rates and cheap transatlantic flights have presented the American holiday paradise with a boom in tourists from the 'old countries' the likes of which it has never known. In general, two weeks in Florida can be booked for the same price as two weeks in the Canaries, except during the high winter season; moreover a holiday in the Sunshine State can offer much more variety with the right planning, and the great advantage of giving everyone the chance to find their own idyllic beach far away from the crowds. What is to stop you hopping over the Atlantic?

For British visitors, the average eight-hour flight to Miami might be off-putting. The reward waiting at the other end, however, is a holiday land almost unrivalled in its perfection. Florida really does have mile after mile of glorious beaches, and sunshine guaranteed to tan on over 330 days a year. A T-shirt should still be packed in 'winter', with temperatures at around 64°F/18°C. Florida is not only a combination of sun and sea, but also of lively beach activity, idyllic palm shores, excellent scuba-diving areas, Mickey Mouse and Disney World, round-the-clock entertainment, frenetic night-life, the glittering Miami skyline and the unique natural spectacle of the Everglades and its alligators.

Florida boasts nearly 1,500 miles of coastline on the Atlantic Ocean and the Gulf of Mexico, and no point in Florida is further than 80 miles from the sea. The water temperatures are warm enough for year-round bathing. The beaches around Miami on the Atlantic coast are world famous and accordingly well frequented. By contrast, the Lee Island Coast around Fort Myers is the local tip for a more relaxing holiday.

Visitors planning a beach holiday in the Sunshine State have the choice between the Atlantic Ocean and the Gulf of Mexico; both coasts have their advantages and disadvantages. Generally, the Gulf coast is quieter, less developed and considerably more expensive than the Atlantic coast between Miami Beach, Fort Lauderdale and West Palm Beach, where a surplus of accommodation, particularly in the less popular summer season, has forced down the prices. The water quality on both coasts is good, as the strict American environmental regulations prohibit the discharge of toxic effluent in seas and rivers.

Is Florida the package-holiday destination of the 90s? It is certainly not cheap, but definitely a rewarding investment. Florida is a holiday paradise not only for its natural attractions but also, and above all, for its leisure facilities. To coin a phrase: Florida's got the lot. This applies as much to sporting activities, predominantly aquatic sports – scuba diving, deep-sea fishing and all types of boating – as to entertainment.

Orlando is the gateway to the most sought-after attraction in the country: Disney World and the adjoining Epcot Center, where the 'Future World' display offers a glimpse of life in the future in a most entertaining and technically ingenious way. Disney World, Walt Disney's second brainchild, which was opened in 1971, is at 98 acres a third larger than its famous predecessor, Disneyland in California, and is one of the largest complexes of its kind in the world. It is a world of make-believe where you can say hello to Mickey Mouse as you walk around.

Tomorrow's world can be experienced today at nearby Cape Canaveral. It was from here that the first men took off to the moon. Nowadays it is the launch site for the Space Shuttle. By way of contrast, one of Florida's oldest attractions is Cypress Gardens. This tropical park near Tampa, famous for its hourly waterskiing shows, is worth at least one day's trip. It is a huge botanical garden through which visitors may wander on foot or take the electric boat on one of the many canals.

Visitors who would prefer something more sophisticated, who are lovers of night-life but do not wish to miss out on the beach, will feel at home in the mecca of the smart set, Miami, and Miami Beach a few miles away. Here night can be turned into day if required, and it is the place to bump into a film star or two. The metropolis offers many forms of entertainment to suit every taste and pocket. Downtown Miami, characterised by its towering office-blocks and luxury hotels, is typically American; its Art Deco district is not as well known. Comprising some 800 buildings in the Art Deco style of the 1930s, it represents the largest single concentration of

Art Deco District, Miami

this architectural style in any city of the world.

The Everglades National Park south-west of Miami offers a wonderful encounter with wildlife. The swampland, its banks fringed with mangroves, is the habitat of many species of birds including osprey, pelicans and flamingos. The alligators may also be admired, from the safety of a boat. The 37-mile-long Park Road gives access to most of the park's attractions.

Last but not least there are the 'Keys', the little islands which extend like a string of pearls from the southern tip of Florida. They are connected by forty-two bridges and end at Key West, where both Ernest Hemingway and Tennessee Williams lived for many years. The Ernest Hemingway Museum, one of many preserved historic houses, is open to the public. Visitors to Key West should forget the time, and, after a relaxing day, settle down to enjoy the musicians, dancers and magicians who perform on Mallory Pier in the evening. This is a place for romantics, and worth savouring.

The list of sights does not end here by any means, and this is merely an appetiser for your holiday in the land of endless possibilities. The 'Florida Attraction Association' has compiled over fifty recommended sights for tourists and the list is growing every year. One trip alone is hardly enough to see all the sights in the Sunshine State; the only thing that Florida cannot offer its guests is boredom.

Essential details in brief

Florida:
The Sunshine State takes its name from the Spanish *'pascua florida'* – a few days after Easter – when the Spanish explorer Ponce de León first set foot there in 1513.

Area:
At approx. 58,687 sq miles Florida covers 1.6% of the total area of the USA. Its coasts are bordered by the Atlantic Ocean in the east and the Gulf of Mexico in the west. Florida extends for over 620 miles from north to south; its average breadth is 137 miles.

Administration:
In 1822 Florida became one of the United States territories, but officially entered the Union as the 27th state only 23 years later. Tallahassee is the state capital of Florida. Its governing body consists of the Senate, with 40 members, and the House of Representatives with 119 members. Florida is made up of 67 administrative regions (counties), overseen by the governor and six ministers.

Population:
Although relatively small in area, Florida has the sixth highest state population in the USA at 13 million. The population is growing as the Sunshine State is still the most popular retirement area for wealthy Americans. 82% of the population live in cities; some 14% are black, a lower proportion than in other southern states. As well as Indian and Asian minorities, many Cuban immigrants have settled in the state and they make up 10% of the population.

Topography:
In the south the land is flat with extensive swamps; in the central area and to the north the land is hilly, to a maximum height of 340 ft. The entire Gulf coast is rich in bays and lagoons; the endless sandy beaches of the Atlantic coast adjoin the Everglades swampland to the south.

Coastline:
Florida's coastline is 1,490 miles long; this extends to 11,178 miles with the addition of bays and the Keys.

Borders:
Florida has only two neighbouring states: Alabama and Georgia. To the south, the 93-mile-wide Straits of Florida separate the state from Cuba.

Pleasure Island, Walt Disney World

Life in Florida

Sunshine, beaches and blue sea; never-ending orange-plantations; Walt Disney with Goofy and Mickey Mouse; affluent American senior citizens spending their retirement playing golf and strolling in the perpetual springtime. Among all this is an army of sun-starved tourists, who, thanks to the state of the dollar, are arriving in increasing numbers from overseas to be pampered by high standards of service. This is the best side of Florida.

The other, shadier side is not mentioned in the glossy travel brochures but appears every day in the newspapers. Drug-related crime is rapidly increasing and gang warfare within the drug mafia is becoming more violent. There is a booming drug trade in Miami in particular; three quarters of the cocaine and heroin confiscated by the authorities in the USA is seized here. Miami has adopted the sombre reputation of the Chicago of the 1920s; certain city districts should be avoided after dark.

There are also problems out in the country, where increasing poverty in the low-income bracket is becoming more widespread as the farming industry tackles market crises. The billions earned through tourism mostly return to the big investors. Nevertheless Florida belongs among the three richest states of the USA, a fact which does not surprise any visitor to the well-maintained suburbs, the lavish leisure facilities and the National Parks, which are perfectly adapted for tourism.

The Sunshine State has never lacked finance since the pioneering days when the industrial and railway magnates Henry Morrison Flagler and Henry Plant constructed a railroad through the state to Key West. In the beginning almost the whole economy was based on agriculture; by virtue of its favourable geographical position and equally good infrastructure, Florida became the supplier of citrus fruits to the nation, which it has remained to this day. The farmers' main source of income is from oranges, though competition on the world market in the last three years has had a negative effect on this particular sector. Other sources of income are vegetables, tobacco, peanuts and sugar cane; Florida has been the biggest supplier of sugar cane in the USA since the economic boycott of Cuba.

The income from agriculture in 1989 was around a billion dollars, an insignificant amount compared with the 12 billions earned from tourism in the same period. Florida would certainly rank as an economically depressed area in the USA without the revenue from tourism: every second inhabitant's income is directly or indirectly dependent on the holiday trade. Almost 60% of the population are engaged in service industries and the numbers are growing. Statistically, every income in Florida increases 50% faster than the national average and new jobs are created twice as quickly.

Rich Americans have always liked to soak up the sun in the extreme southeastern state. The first hesitant steps towards organising tourism for the sunseekers were already being taken at the end of the last century. The great boom came in the 1920s when in Miami Beach alone almost 500 hotels and apartment blocks were erected in one year. Shortly afterwards the hotel developers discovered the Gulf coast, concentrating at first on the St Petersburg area. Up to the outbreak of the Second World War 2.5 million tourists per year were recorded in Florida. Since then the number has increased tenfold.

In terms of area Florida is comparatively small, but boasts the third largest population of all the United States. The state embodies the dream of American prosperity to which mass tourism has been a major contributing factor from 1971. It was at that time that Walt Disney opened Disney World. The extent of its attractions overshadowed those of its famous predecessor in California. Donald Duck & co brought 70,000 hotel beds to Orlando (formerly a small provincial town), which are booked almost all year round. An extra boost was provided by the Epcot Center which was added ten years later. As everything seems to be running very smoothly at present, the next investors are standing in line and new fantasy worlds are being planned. For instance, the film giants Universal Studios have invested a few hundred million dollars in a film theme-park in the Disney mould. If this trend continues, the last orange-tree will have to make way in the foreseeable future for the holiday industry.

Signposts of history

About 8000 BC: First settlement by Indian peoples.

About 600 BC: Nomadic hunting tribes establish permanent settlements. First traces of land cultivation.

AD 1513: The Spaniard Juan Ponce de León discovers the peninsula on Easter Sunday and names it Florida after the Spanish for the Easter period, *pascua florida*.

1521: Spanish settlers establish a colony at Punta Gorda on the Gulf of Mexico, but the settlement is not permanent.

1539: Hernando de Soto claims Florida for Spain.

1565: St Augustine is founded, the oldest town in the USA.

17th and 18th c: Conflicts between Spain, France and England for possession of Florida.

1763: Florida becomes a British territory.

1783: Spanish troops use the American War of Independence to their advantage and regain Florida.

1817–18: The native Indians try unsuccessfully to expel the white invaders. First of the Seminole Wars.

1818: The USA tries to take Florida from Spain. General Andrew Jackson conquers Pensacola.

1821: Spain surrenders and sells Florida to the USA for 5 million dollars.

1822: Florida becomes a territory of the United States.

1824: Tallahassee is designated the capital of the new territory.

1835: Beginning of the second Seminole War.

1842: The Seminole Indians are defeated after seven years' bloody conflict. Most of the surviving native population are expelled to Oklahoma.

1845: Florida enters the Union as the 27th state. The population is 58,000.

1855–58: The last few hundred Seminole Indians tackle the US army in a desperate and hopeless battle and are virtually annihilated. There are only a few small Reservations in Florida today.

1861–65: During the American Civil War Florida is allied to the southern Confederate states, but there is little military action on the peninsula.

End of 19th c: The entrepreneurs Henry Flagler and Henry Plant develop Florida by building railroads. Extensive citrus plantations and winter-vegetable cultivation are established. At the turn of the century the population has risen to 500,000.

1950: Construction of the 'Spaceport' at Cape Canaveral begins; later renamed Kennedy Space Center.

1960 onwards: First influx of Cuban refugees, which continues to the present day.

1969: The astronauts Neil Armstrong, Edwin Aldrin and Michael Collins take off from Cape Canaveral in Apollo 11 and make history when Armstrong and Aldrin are the first men on the moon.

1970: Florida is officially elected the Sunshine State.

1971: Disney World opens.

1981: First launch of the Space Shuttle.

1986: The Space Shuttle Challenger explodes on take-off.

Food and drink – a guide for overseas visitors

In Florida's restaurants you will be introduced to the culinary diversity of all its ethnic groups; the neighbouring states and an influx of Cubans have greatly influenced the local cuisine.

There are typical American restaurants where a 'host' or 'hostess' will show you to your table and the steaks are excellent. Seafood dishes, including lobster, crayfish, crabs, scampi and shrimps, can be found on the menu in all possible variations. Local specialities include *conch chowder* (shellfish soup), *stone crab* and *turf 'n' surf* (steak with king prawns). People with extra-large appetites should go to an *all-you-can-eat seafood restaurant* or to one of the major restaurant chains. The food is often very good in one of the *Raw Bars* usually situated near the harbour, where the *catch of the day*, advertised on a board, is worth noting (e.g. *red snapper*, *mullet* or *dolphin* – which in fact is not dolphin at all).

Breakfast

Breakfast is taken in a Coffee Shop and consists of a traditional cooked meal starting with fresh orange-juice and cereal, followed by fried, boiled, poached or scrambled eggs (fried eggs are prepared 'sunny side up' and 'over', or fried both sides, and medium or well done), served with bacon, ham or sausages and *hashed brown potatoes* (potato pancakes). Toast and marmalade, pancakes with maple syrup or the popular *Dunkin Donuts* complete the meal. Coffee-cups are constantly refilled at no extra charge.

Lunch

In the USA lunch is usually a quick snack of sandwiches or a hamburger; whatever it

Crab claws – Palm Beach

is, it has to be quick. Try the *special of the day* in one of the numerous fast-food restaurants (no alcoholic beverages served), or go to a Cuban snack bar. Soup and salads are often on the midday menus.

Dinner

By contrast, dinner has a more alcoholic flavour, starting usually with a couple of Martinis or Bloody Marys. Many Americans continue to drink these powerful cocktails during their main meal. Hors d'oeuvres are usually ignored in favour of sampling the generous salad buffet as often as desired; there is always a choice of dressings. Bread and butter are included at no extra charge.

Apart from international cuisine and seafood specialities, steak and chicken are the main dishes in American restaurants. As a rule, Americans like to eat their steaks rare and this is how they will be prepared unless you instruct otherwise. Baked potato with sour cream is the usual side-dish. Chicken is almost always fried in breadcrumbs.

Dessert

Most of the desserts are high-calorie affairs: hot fudge sundae and banana split are among the favourites. Florida's own speciality is *Key Lime Pie*, a rich mixture of condensed milk, eggs, lime-juice and sugar, baked and then served cold. There are always ample supplies of fresh fruit.

Drinks

Beer is the most common beverage; the major brands are sold in bars, restaurants and even petrol stations, sometimes on draught but usually in cans and bottles. American beer is not as strong as European lagers and is served very cold. Iced tea with lemon is very refreshing and served everywhere. Those who prefer to drink wine will find excellent Californian wines available in Florida; they are comparable in quality to European wines.

Cocktails and rum-based mixed drinks (*Planter's Punch*, *Pina Colada*, *Daiquiris*, etc.) are very popular, very good, but dangerously deceptive as the taste often disguises the alcohol content.

Three drinks from Florida

Pina Colada

A strong rather than sweet version of this well-known cocktail:

Put in a shaker 1 measure of brown rum (c. 60%), 2 measures of white rum, 2 measures of pineapple juice and 4 measures of coconut milk, and mix well. Fill up two-thirds of a glass or hollow coconut-shell with crushed ice and pour in the cocktail. Serve with a straw.

Seminole Cocktail

This recipe was discovered in a bar on the outskirts of one of the Indian reservations in Florida:

Put in a shaker 1 measure of Campari, 1 measure of Vodka, 2 measures of passion-fruit juice, ¼ measure of fresh lemon-juice and a dash of Angostura Bitters, and mix well. Serve over crushed ice in a glass.

'Florida Keys'

Recommended by Harry, a barman in Key West (his favourite recipe):

Mix 1 measure of blue Curaçao and 4 measures of Californian or European extra-dry sparkling wine. Dip the rim of a champagne glass in sugar and chill. Pour in the cocktail and garnish with a thick slice of orange.

Hints for your holiday: for overseas visitors

Some like it hot, so they jet across the Atlantic in July and August and are surprised just how hot it can be. Even the temperatures in the shade at this time of year in Florida are only just bearable under a coconut palm on the beach in the constant sea breeze. Sunburn has ruined many a holiday here in no time at all. A glance at the map will show that the south of the Sunshine State extends into a subtropical region, where winters are seldom cooler than 68°F/20°C and summer temperatures often exceed 90°F/32°C. It is a different story in the north, where sudden frost can spoil bathing holidays and fruit harvests alike. The best time to visit Florida is in the spring and autumn. People with plenty of money to spare can spend a very comfortable winter in the deep south, a fact which drives both the number of North American tourists and the prices to extremes between December and March.

Seminole Indian

'Sun and fun' is the motto in Florida. The perfect holiday machine is in motion everywhere, whether in Disney World or Key West, Pinellas Suncoast or Miami Beach. Nowhere else in the USA are there as many hotels, restaurants, pleasure parks and interesting (often artificially created) sights as in Florida. As regards food, the better restaurants, though still very expensive, have earned their status since the trend moved away from the McDonald's and Kentucky Fried Chicken format towards the cuisines of France, Italy or Mexico. The hamburger, of course, still plays a vital role as a reasonably priced, if not downright cheap, meal, is available on every street corner and can usually be served direct to your car window.

A car is an absolute necessity when visiting Florida. There are great distances between beach hotels and shopping centres, amusement parks and restaurants. It is advisable to book hotel accommodation in advance and to hire a car for the holiday. The car-hire rates here are still the lowest in the world. If the rental is not arranged before departure, it is advisable to take a credit card if possible. It is the normal method of payment here and all major cards are accepted. A credit card saves you having to leave a sizeable deposit when you hire a car.

A final word of advice: don't forget to tip; waiters and waitresses earn their wages this way. 10–15% of the final bill is usual for service.

Miami Beach

Where to go and what to see

The east coast

Lying on Florida's east coast are the big-name attractions of Key West, Miami, Fort Lauderdale, Palm Beach and Daytona where the majority of visitors to Florida spend their holidays. The John Pennekamp Coral Reef State Park is an underwater Garden of Eden, an almost 125-mile-long coral reef lying parallel to the Florida Keys. The Keys are divided into the Upper Keys from Key Largo, the largest island, to Long Key; the Middle Keys extending to Seven Mile Bridge; and the Lower Keys to Key West.

25 miles from Key Largo lies the Everglades National Park, a unique swampland environment of rare species of flora and fauna, which stretches over the entire southern tip of Florida. This fragile wilderness is only accessible by road from the east coast. There is a succession of resorts from Key West to Fernandina Beach.

The Florida Keys

The twenty-nine islands which extend between the Atlantic and the Gulf of Mexico from the southern tip of Florida towards Cuba are the Florida Keys, the jewel of the Sunshine State. The magic of the Caribbean starts here: tropical vegetation, white beaches, picture-book sunsets, hot rhythms and cool drinks. It is a paradise for fishing and watersports.

The Keys should be explored by car; the *Overseas Highway* itself is an unforgettable experience. This 113-mile highway links all the islands and crosses forty-two bridges. A tip when driving from *Florida City* is to take a short detour via the *Card Sound Toll Bridge* rather than the usual route on US Highway 1, as the scenery is more impressive.

Anglers and brown pelican, Florida

Key Largo Pop. 3,000

The largest of the Keys achieved fame in the film of the same name starring Humphrey Bogart and Lauren Bacall. Its real-life criminal past goes back as far as the 17th and 18th c. when Caribbean pirates used it as a hideout. Nowadays the island is a centre for fishing and diving. Many of the diving equipment shops offer short diving courses locally on the only living coral reef on the American continent. The *Overseas Highway*, completed in 1938, begins at Key Largo and extends down to Key West almost exclusively on bridges. The *New York Times* enthusiastically described it at the time as the 'highway that goes to sea'.

 Small sand and shingle beaches.

 Several schools, and equipment hire.

 Key Largo Campground with all facilities.

✈ Excursion flights over the Keys with Coral Reef Flying Services, Port Largo Airport.

Key Largo

A special tip

The USA's first underwater national park, the *John Pennekamp Coral Reef State Park* extends over 130 sq miles. This fascinating underwater world can be explored without full scuba gear as some of the coral reefs reach up almost to the water's surface. There are daily scuba and snorkelling tours and trips in glass-bottomed boats.

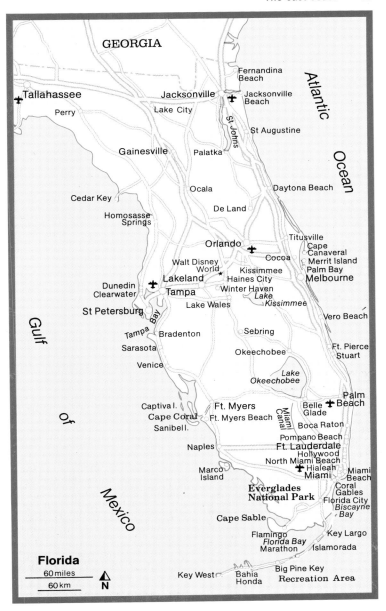

GEORGIA

Atlantic

Ocean

Tallahassee

Perry

Fernandina
Beach

Jacksonville

Jacksonville
Beach

Lake City

St Augustine

St Johns

Gainesville

Palatka

Ocala

Daytona Beach

Cedar Key

De Land

Homosasse
Springs

Titusville
Cape
Canaveral
Merrit Island
Palm Bay
Melbourne

Orlando

Walt Disney
World

Cocoa

Kissimmee

Dunedin
Clearwater

Lakeland

Haines City

Tampa

Winter Haven

Lake
Kissimmee

St Petersburg

Lake Wales

Tampa Bay

Bradenton

Vero Beach

Sarasota

Sebring

Okeechobee

Ft. Pierce
Stuart

Venice

Lake
Okeechobee

Captiva I.
Cape Coral
Sanibel I.

Ft. Myers
Ft. Myers Beach

Belle
Glade

Palm
Beach

Miami Canal

Boca Raton

Naples

Pompano Beach
Ft. Lauderdale
Hollywood
North Miami Beach
Hialeah

Marco
Island

Miami
Beach

Miami

Everglades
National Park

Coral
Gables
Florida City
Biscayne
Bay

Cape Sable

Flamingo
Florida Bay
Marathon

Key Largo

Islamorada

Florida

60 miles

60 km

N

Key West

Bahia
Honda

Big Pine Key
Recreation Area

Gulf

of

Mexico

Upper Matecumbe Pop. 1,500

The town of *Islamorada* on Upper Matecumbe is one of the most important resorts on the Keys. The town is the base of the largest charter fleet for deep-sea fishing. The best beaches in the Keys are to be found nearby. The *Theater of the Sea* to the north with its dolphin and sea-lion displays is well worth seeing.

 Several good beaches.

Long Key

Sea World's Shark Institute in *Layton City* is definitely worth a visit. All types of sharks found in the waters off Florida can be observed here at close quarters.

Vaca Key Pop. 8,000

Marathon on Vaca Key is the largest town on the islands after Key West. Together with neighbouring *Key Colony Beach*, it is one of the main holiday centres and offers all amenities.

 Several good beaches.

 Sombrero Golf Course (18 holes).

 Marathon has three shopping centres.

 Daily flights from Marathon to Key West and Miami, also excursion flights.

Bahia Honda Key

The island is a nature conservation area, the *Bahia Honda State Park*. There are no hotels, but there is a beautifully located campsite and the only naturist beach on the Keys. Like Upper Matecumbe, Bahia Honda is an ideal spot for water-lovers, with picturesque palm beaches, diving schools and boat hire.

Big Pine Key

The *National Key Deer Refuge* is the home of a unique native species of deer, the *white tail Key deer*, somewhat smaller in size than an adult Alsatian dog.

Key West Pop. 50,000

Key West is the southernmost town of the continental USA and occupies almost the whole of its island. Both Ernest Hemingway and Tennessee Williams lived and found their inspiration here. Harry S. Truman, 33rd president of the United States, migrated regularly from Washington to Key West in the winter and governed from the *Little White House*. There is a special atmosphere in Key West: narrow streets, picturesque old colonial-style houses, pleasant cafés and a colourful medley of people from all walks of life, from beachcombers to multi-millionaires.

 During the Spanish occupation the island was named *Cayo Hueso* (Bone Island), which possibly referred to the terrible massacre of Indian natives here. In 1822 naval lieutenant Matthew C. Perry claimed the island for the USA. The Americans established a base and stationed over 1,000 soldiers at Key West in an effort to combat piracy. The town grew rapidly and became a centre of the cigar industry. Henry Flagler constructed a railroad to Key West in 1912 and had a large hotel built. The railway was taken out of operation in 1935; today the old rails can be seen supporting some of the bridges.

What to see

The best way to get an impression of the sights is to take the 13-mile tour on the

Right: Colonial house, Key West

Conch Tour Train lasting 1½ hours. The recommended sights are:

Mallory Square and Pier: countless people gather every evening at the harbour to watch the sunset and the street players.

The Wreckers' Museum (322 Duval Street): displays all aspects of the wreckers' business of plundering stranded ships.

Oldest House Museum (same block): erected in 1832, this is the oldest preserved house in Key West and is furnished in early 19th c. style.

Spanish Treasure Ship (633 Front Street): the reconstruction of the Spanish galleon *Nuestra Señora de Atocha*. The search for the wreck and its exact reconstruction cost three lives and 2 million dollars. Open to the public daily 9.30 am to 5.30 pm.

The Lighthouse (938 Whitehead Street): the old lighthouse affords a magnificent panoramic view of the island. The telescope is the periscope of a Japanese submarine sunk during the attack on Pearl Harbour. There is an adjoining naval museum.

Hemingway House

Hemingway House (907 Whitehead Street): Ernest Hemingway wrote his masterpiece *The Old Man and the Sea* in this villa in the 1930s. The house and garden are open to the public.

Audubon House & Gardens (Whitehead/ Greene Streets): this was the home at the beginning of the 19th c. of the famous artist John James Audubon, whose main interest was the birdlife of the Keys.

Mel Fisher's Treasure Exhibit (Greene/ Front Streets): something for treasure-hunters: gold, silver and equipment recovered from two Spanish galleons sunk in 1622.

East Martello Tower (3500 South Roosevelt Boulevard): a historical museum.

Peggy Mills Gardens: this is how the extreme south of the archipelago must have looked long ago. Palm-trees, fig-trees, mahogany and numerous exotic plants may be admired in this beautifully situated park.

A special tip

The *Key West Cigar Factory* in Pirates Alley is the only cigar factory still in production and is a one-man business. There George Culmer will roll you a Havana.

 Good sandy beaches; no changing cubicles or showers on the public beaches.

 Boat trips and tours in glass-bottomed boats.

 Ray's Bike Shop, Truman Avenue.

Lime-trees grow wild in Key West's gardens. Try the sweet Key Lime Pie.

Alligator on the Anhinga Trail

Everglades National Park

Of the 3,860 sq miles of swampland which extend over Florida's southern tip, 2,120 sq miles belong to the Everglades National Park, an expanse of water, wind and grass. 'Ever Glades' was the name which appeared on the first map, and was a corruption of the name 'River Glades' given to the area by a land surveyor. The plain, covered in high cladium grass (sawgrass) and interlaced by countless waterways, is the habitat of alligators, over 300 species of birds and over 600 species of fish. Nature-lovers can explore the park by car, by canoe or on foot. Airboat trips are only available outside the National Park area, around Miccosukee on US Highway 41, 25 miles west of Miami. The only access road to the park is from the east via

 The famous tippler Hemingway is a selling point throughout Key West, first and foremost at Sloppy Joe's Saloon where the Planter's Punch really *does* pack a punch.

 Daily greyhound races at *Key West Kennel Club, Stock Island.*

 Concerts by well-known American pop, rock and folk bands are held regularly in various clubs and halls.

Key West has an array of elegant shops. The *Key West Fragrance & Cosmetic Factory* (524 Front Street) is quite exceptional and sells reasonably priced cosmetics based on Aloe extract. The hand-printed fabrics at the *Key West Handprint Fabrics Factory* (529 Front Street) are also inexpensive.

 Daily air service to Marathon and Miami.

Ex Take the sea-plane to *Fort Jefferson*, the largest brick-built fortress in the western world, on *Garden Key* in the *Dry Tortugas* islands, 69 miles west of Key West.

The Anhinga Trail

Mangrove swamp in the Everglades

Homestead. There is also access by sea from the west coast via Everglades City. However you choose to get there, be sure to allow plenty of time, at least two days, to explore the beauty of the Everglades.

Visitors to the National Park are warned to keep to the official marked footpaths and marked waterways for canoeing; these routes are, in brief:

Long Pine Key Nature Trail: 7 miles through pine forests.

Pa-hay-okee Trail: the 435-yd-long boardwalk leads to an observation platform for a view across the swamp grass. This is the habitat not only of many species of birds, but also of watersnakes and rattlesnakes, though these are rarely seen.

Anhinga Trail: 875 yds, the most interesting trail. The boardwalks cross waters in which alligators, snakes, fish and hundreds of aquatic birds can be seen. Don't forget to take your camera!

Gumbo Limbo Trail: 875 yds, with royal palms, gumbo limbo trees and many climbing plants.

Mahogany Hammock Trail: 875 yds, with the largest mahogany-trees in the USA.

Taking a canoe trip through the Everglades offers closer views of the scenery. Canoes can be hired in the *Flamingo Visitor Center*, and there are three canoe trails: *Hells Bay Canoe Trail*, *West Lake* and *Bear Lake Canoe Trail*. (Motorboats can also be hired from the Visitor Center.)

There is only one hotel, at the Flamingo Visitor Center. It is advisable to reserve accommodation during the high season (November to April). Tel. (813) 695 3101.

A licence is required for freshwater fishing (obtainable from the Visitor Center).

Campsites at Flamingo and Long Pine Key, and numerous more basic sites in the park; apply to the Park Ranger.

Visitors should try to call in at the Main Visitor Center at the park entrance where there are films, maps and brochures and an exhibition. Daily guided tours from the Royal Palm Visitor Center at 10 am and 3 pm. The best time to visit the park is between November and April; in summer it is hot, humid and rainy and there are swarms of insects.

Ex Excursion tours through the park in open vehicles leave from the Visitor Center.

Miami/Miami Beach
Pop. 478,000

The twin cities of Miami (pop. 380,000) and Miami Beach (98,000) are constantly expanding. Greater Miami, with a population of 2 million, is the largest conurbation in Florida. You can already feel the Caribbean atmosphere of this meeting-point with Latin America when you arrive at the international airport. Almost a million Cubans and other Hispanics who live here have brought youth to a city which had long been regarded as the retirement home of America.

The lively, hectic metropolis is an important commercial centre, an exciting melting-pot of diverse nationalities – and a centre for drug trafficking. The billions made from the flourishing drug trade are accumulating in the banks. The TV series *Miami Vice* has focused attention on the city and stimulated its economic growth.

Miami's history can be summarised very briefly. Its name comes from the Calusa Indians who called the area *Mayami* (Great Water). Miami was a sleepy township with an Indian trading-post until 1896, when the construction of the railroad brought about its economic development. Miami Beach became a holiday resort some decades later when the industrialist Carl Fisher had the mangrove swamps drained to create building land.

What to see in Miami

Miami is divided into a strict grid of streets. The Avenues and Courts run from north to south in broad lines, and between them the Streets or Terraces branch off at right angles like rungs on a ladder. The street names tell you which area you are in, e.g. NW 42 Ave.

Miami and Miami Beach are sepa-

Miami

rated by *Biscayne Bay* and linked by five causeways. Luxury liners head off to the Bahamas and the Caribbean from the largest cruise port in the world. The 8-mile-long holiday island of Miami Beach is also known as the American Riviera.

To gain a first impression of Miami, visitors should make a circuit of the Metromover, an elevated rail system which circles Downtown Miami in only ten minutes. The sight of this expanding city's skyline glittering gold in the sunset is unequalled. At Government Center Station you can change to the Metrorail rapid transit or to the Metrobuses.

Metro Dade Cultural Center
(101 W Flagler Street): The new Spanish-style cultural centre is renowned for exhibitions of modern art. The complex contains a library, an arts centre with a frequently changing programme of temporary exhibitions, and the *Historical Museum of South Florida* offering a good survey of Florida's history.

Little Havana
The legendary Cuban quarter lying between the inner city and Coral Gables is considered the secret heart of Miami. It is concentrated around Calle Ocho (8th Street). Strolling along its streets, you can take in the colourful hustle and bustle, visit a factory where cigars are still rolled by hand, or sit in one of the pleasant cafés and try a cup of 'café cubano' or one of the other Cuban specialities.

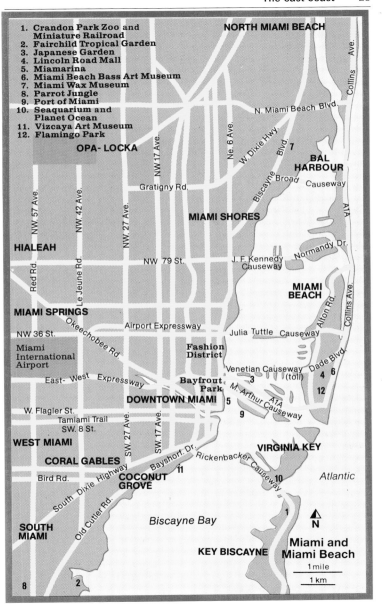

1. Crandon Park Zoo and
   Miniature Railroad
2. Fairchild Tropical Garden
3. Japanese Garden
4. Lincoln Road Mall
5. Miamarina
6. Miami Beach Bass Art Museum
7. Miami Wax Museum
8. Parrot Jungle
9. Port of Miami
10. Seaquarium and
    Planet Ocean
11. Vizcaya Art Museum
12. Flamingo Park

NORTH MIAMI BEACH

Collins Ave.

OPA-LOCKA

NE. 6 Ave.

N. Miami Beach Blvd.

W. Dixie Hwy.

Biscayne Blvd.

7

BAL HARBOUR

Broad Causeway

NW. 17 Ave.

Gratigny Rd.

MIAMI SHORES

A1A

NW. 57 Ave.

NW. 42 Ave.

NW. 27 Ave.

HIALEAH

Red Rd.

Le Jeune Rd.

Okeechobee Rd.

NW 79 St.

J. F. Kennedy Causeway

Normandy Dr.

MIAMI BEACH

MIAMI SPRINGS

Airport Expressway

Julia Tuttle Causeway

Alton Rd.

Collins Ave.

NW 36 St.

Miami International Airport

Fashion District

Venetian Causeway (toll)

Dade Blvd.

4

6

3

12

East- West Expressway

Bayfront Park

5

M. Arthur Causeway

A1A

DOWNTOWN MIAMI

9

W. Flagler St.

Tamiami Trail

SW. 8 St.

SW. 27 Ave.

SW. 17 Ave.

WEST MIAMI

VIRGINIA KEY

CORAL GABLES

Bird Rd.

Bayshort. Dr.

Rickenbacker Causeway

10

Atlantic

South Dixie Highway

COCONUT GROVE

11

SOUTH MIAMI

Old Cutler Rd.

Biscayne Bay

1

N

KEY BISCAYNE

Miami and Miami Beach

8

2

1 mile

1 km

Vizcaya Museum
Seaquarium

Vizcaya Museum

(3251 South Miami Avenue): The millionaire James Deering had this Italian-style villa built in 1916. For five years some 1,000 craftsmen worked on the furnishings and decoration of the rooms in Renaissance, Baroque, Rococo and Neoclassical styles. The villa stands in an extensive park with fountains and small lakes.

Downtown Miami

The skyline of downtown Miami, an area of gigantic shopping centres, is characterised by its ultra-modern glass palaces which throw bizarre reflections. The Cen-Trust building, through which the Metromover runs, is a shining example of the new generation of skyscrapers. The Atlantis residential complex on Brickwell Avenue is also impressive.

Bayfront Park

(Biscayne Boulevard): From here there is a breathtaking view over Biscayne Bay. The John F. Kennedy Flame of Friendship burns in the park.

Seaquarium
(4400 Rickenbacker Causeway, Key Biscayne): Trained killer whales and dolphins, with the expertise of 'Flipper' from the TV series, have made the Seaquarium famous. Sea-lions also perform and sharks can be seen feeding in the enormous seawater tank. Continuous shows from 10 am.

Planet Ocean
(3979 Rickenbacker Causeway): Directly opposite is an interesting oceanographic exhibition with a survey of marine history.

Japanese Garden
(MacArthur Causeway), with tea house.

Wax Museum
(13899 Biscayne Boulevard): Over 200 wax figures of well-known personalities are displayed here.

Coral Gables
This Spanish/Mediterranean-style complex was founded by George Edgar Merrick. The main access roads approach Coral Gables through limestone arches named Alhambra, Granada and La Puerta del Sol. The focal point is the exclusive Biltmore Hotel with its 295-ft tower modelled on the Giralda Tower in Seville. There is a golf course directly in front of the hotel.

View from Bayside, Bayfront Park: the Marina and, beyond, the Port of Miami

Coral Gables House
(907 Coral Way): George Merrick's childhood home, built in 1898 from coral rock.

Lowe Art Museum
of the University of Miami (1301 Stanford Drive): Collections of American, European and Oriental art.

Coconut Grove
Miami's artists' and students' quarter has a lively atmosphere. A succession of art galleries, smart boutiques, theatres, and pavement cafés under tropical trees.

Barnacle State Historical Site
(3485 Main Highway): The residence of the architect Munroe who built the first hotel in Coconut Grove. Guided tours on Wednesdays.

Fairchild Tropical Gardens
(1090 Old Cutler Road): A miniature rain forest with thirteen artificial lakes. Train tours hourly.

Parrot Jungle
(11000 SW 57th Avenue): Over 1,000 tropical birds live in this 'jungle'. Most are tame, may be fed by hand, and will perch on visitors' shoulders for souvenir photos.

Miami Metrozoo
(12400 SW 152nd Street): Over 100 animal species roam in the grounds.

Monkey Jungle
(14805 SW 216th Street): Quite an experience! Visitors walk through cages to see hundreds of monkeys roam free outside in a jungle environment.

Spanish Monastery of St Bernard
(16711 West Dixie Highway): The oldest monastery in the USA was originally built in Segovia, Spain, in 1141 and transported stone by stone to Florida in 1925 by the publisher Randolph Hearst. The monastery has been faithfully reconstructed and houses a museum of medieval art.

Serpentarium
(12655 Dixie Highway): Here giant turtles, iguanas, crocodiles and snakes may be admired, and you can watch how cobras are 'milked' of their deadly venom.

Greynolds Park
(West Dixie Highway): A park with barbecue areas and a golf course, boat hire and an observation tower.

 What to see in Miami Beach
The elongated strip of land in the Atlantic has been developed into a resort attracting Americans and Europeans. On Ocean Drive the hotel tower-blocks overlook the sea. The beach is a playground of all nationalities.

Bass Museum of Art
(2100 Collins Avenue): A collection of art ranging from the Middle Ages to the modern period, housed in a superb Art Deco building.

Miami Beach Garden Center and Conservatory
(2000 Convention Center Drive): Tropical flowers and plants, some of which are unique to south Florida.

Art Deco District
(80 blocks and 800 buildings between 6th and 23rd Streets including *Flamingo Park*): On Ocean Drive you could believe you had been transported back in time to the 1920s and '30s. The renovated buildings have Art Deco façades in pale pastel shades and geometric designs, and look most impressive at dusk. Guided walking tours are available from the Miami Design Preservation League (1236 Ocean Drive), an organisation supporting the preservation of the Art Deco District. The biennial

World Art Deco Congress was inaugurated in Miami in 1991.

The great expanse of sand at Miami Beach is a big attraction. Parts are reserved by hotels for their guests, but there are also public access areas.

Bayside Marketplace in downtown Miami (400 Biscayne Boulevard) is one of the most luxurious shopping areas; *Miracle Mall* in Coral Gables (163rd Street) is a giant shopping centre with cinemas. There is an elegant shopping mall at *Bal Harbour Shops* in Coral Gables (Collins Avenue/97th Street), and Mayfair Shops, in Coconut Grove (Grand Avenue/Mary Street), is a shopping arcade in a picturesque atrium.

In winter, top-ranking international stars perform in the big hotels. There are opera performances in the *Dade County Auditorium* (2901 W Flagler Street); theatres include the *Theater of the Performing Arts* (1700 Washington Avenue), *Players State Theater* (3500 Main Highway), *Gusman Center of the Performing Arts* (174 E Flagler Street) and the *University of Miami's Ring Theater* (1380 Miller Drive).

Sports fans will find plenty of distractions here. There is American football with the home team, the Miami Dolphins, at the *Dolphin Stadium* (2269 NW 119th Street); boxing and basketball at the *Miami Beach Convention Center*; and baseball in the *Miami Stadium* (North Miami Avenue/6th and 8th NW Streets). The *Hialeah Park Race Course* (105 E 21st Street) offers an exceptional backdrop to horse-racing: flamingos live in the race course grounds, apparently undisturbed by all the visitors. *Jai Alai*, the fastest ball-game in the world, may be followed from December to April in the *Miami Jai Alai Fronton* (3500 NW 37th Avenue). There is greyhound racing at Biscayne Dog Track (NW 115th Street).

 The *Miami Beach Convention Center* hosts a large annual boat and car show, as well as regular circus performances.

 Motorboat racing may be followed throughout the year at the *Marine Stadium*.

There are no fewer than 34 golf courses in the Miami area.

If you want to catch your own fish, fishing is permitted on the *MacArthur and Rickenbacker Causeways* and from piers at *Haulover Beach Park, South Beach, Sunny Isles* and in *Coconut Grove*. There are yacht-chartering facilities, or you can join a fishing party.

 Florida's holiday capital boasts over 4,000 restaurants. Cuban specialities in Little Havana include *ceviche* (raw fish marinated in lemon-juice); prawns with roasted plantains, *moros y cristianos* (black beans with rice) and *churros* (sweet spiral-shaped fritters). At the *Surfside Beach Hotel* (Miami Beach, 8701 Collins Avenue) you can dine in a luxurious Cadillac. Top-class international cuisine is available in all the *Fontainebleau Hilton's* various restaurants, which are very good but extremely expensive.

A special tip

A sightseeing flight over Miami and surroundings in an airship is an interesting experience; however, the tours do not take place every day. For information contact *Goodyear Blimp Tour, Opa Locka Airport*.

✈ *Miami International Airport* lies to the west of the city and is used by all the major American and European airlines. There are direct links from Miami to many American cities and daily services to South America and the Caribbean. There are helicopter excursion flights from *Watson Island Park.*

Ex The many different boat tours on the *Intracoastal Waterway*, across *Biscayne Bay*, to *Fort Lauderdale* and to the *Everglades*, are all of interest. There are also airboat trips to an island camp of the *Miccosukee Indians* 3 miles west of Miami. The most pleasant boat trip by far is on the *Island Queen*, a Mississippi paddle-steamer. There are also one- to four-day mini-cruises to the *Bahamas* and *Caribbean islands*. Miami is the main port of departure for extended cruises; its harbour can handle 14 cruise ships simultaneously.

Popular mainland excursions include *Pompano Beach*, 20 minutes' drive north of Miami, which has three main attractions: the *Science Museum and Planetarium* with adjoining botanical garden; *Lion Country Safari*, a drive-through safari park with African big game, and a marine theme-park, *Krakatoa*, where a man-made 'active' volcano is the centrepiece. There is also *Water Kingdom* at Hollywood (large water-chutes, waterskiing shows), *Orchid Jungle* at Homestead (orchids displayed in their natural setting) and *Coral Castle*, north on US Highway 1, a castle hewn from the coral reef.

Key Biscayne

The island of Key Biscayne is 3½ miles long, lies to the south of Miami Beach and may be reached from downtown Miami on the *Rickenbacker Causeway*. Key Biscayne has a totally different atmosphere to Miami Beach; the pace here is not as hectic. The island is less developed, has more open spaces and less crowded beaches, but can still offer all the amenities for an action-packed holiday. The main attraction is the *Bill Baggs Cape Florida State Park* on the southern tip of the island, with an old lighthouse. Its observation platform (130 steps) offers wonderful panoramic views of the island and coastline. *The Florida White House*, on the same route, was once the holiday retreat of former US President Richard Nixon and is also open to the public. *Crandon Park* is the southernmost zoo of the continental USA, with over 1,000 animals and a special children's zoo. Children under 13 admitted free.

 Extensive sandy beach.

Fort Lauderdale Pop. 155,000

Young people flock to Fort Lauderdale, particularly in spring when American students from the north are on vacation. This is a city which is 'open all hours'. The promenade is thronged with people into the early hours of the morning. There are however other attractions in Fort Lauderdale. 250 man-made canals cross the city, which has been called the 'Venice of America'. There are miles of sandy beach and beautiful white villas set in colourful tropical gardens. *Port Everglades* to the south-east of the city is a cruise port to the Bahamas and a harbour for luxury yachts.

The city's name tells its story. Major William Lauderdale had a fort constructed here in 1838 during the Seminole War. A small settlement was established under its protection, though it only started to grow rapidly in our own century.

Yachting in Fort Lauderdale

 What to see

The best way to get a first impression of Fort Lauderdale and its sights is to take the 90-minute tour with the *Voyager Sightseeing Train*, or take a boat from *Bahia Mar Marina*.

Ocean World
(1701 SE 17th Street Causeway): Marine aquarium with displays of sea-lions, dolphins, sharks, alligators and turtles.

Gold Coast Railroad
(SW 9th Avenue): A comprehensive railway museum.

Swimming Hall of Fame
(501 Seabreeze Avenue): Hall of fame of world record-holders and Olympic swimming champions.

King Cromartie House
(230 SW 2nd Street): A museum of antiques and furniture records the pioneering days of the turn of the century.

Museum of Art
(Las Olas Boulevard): Classical and modern art from all over the world.

Butterfly World
(Tradewinds Park): Opened in 1989, this is the largest butterfly enclosure in the world. Magnificent butterflies, some the size of plates, can be admired in the large pavilion and may alight on your outstretched hand.

Ocean World, Fort Lauderdale

Ocean Life Viewing Area
(S 17th Street): Interesting ocean aquarium with Atlantic fish species.

 6½ miles of sandy public beaches.

 Las Olas Boulevard is the place for shopping or browsing. The largest shopping centre is the *Galeria* (2500 E Sunrise Boulevard).

 Fort Lauderdale offers all types of summer sports. The popular game of pelota may be followed over dinner in the *Dania Jai Alai Fronton* (301 E Dania Beach Boulevard), as the restaurant has a good view of the pitch. There are trotting-races at *Pompano Park* (Race Track Road).

Pop, rock, folk and jazz dominate the music scene in Fort Lauderdale.

The beachfront restaurants in Fort Lauderdale should be avoided if possible, as they are mass-catering establishments where you may be served steak and ketchup on a plastic plate. A tip for gourmets is the *Café du Beaujolais* (3134 NE 9th Street) where French haute cuisine is served in 1930s-style decor. The *Café de Genève* (1519 South Andrews) specialises in Swiss cheese fondues. *The Ambry* (Commercial Boulevard) is the restaurant of soccer star Gerd Müller, who played for the Fort Lauderdale Strikers between 1978 and 1981. *Lagniappe Cajun House* (3134 NE 9th Street) serves an excellent Sunday brunch to an accompaniment of Dixieland Jazz.

✈ Fort Lauderdale International Airport offers direct flights to many cities in the USA, including neighbouring Miami.

Ex Excursions on the Fort Lauderdale canals; mini-cruises on the *Intracoastal Waterway*; Riverboat Shuffles or dinner trips on the Mississippi steamers *Paddlewheel Queen* and *Jungle Queen*. It is advisable to book in advance, ideally through your hotel. Many tour firms offer day trips to the Everglades. The *Sea Rocket* leaves Dania Beach several times a day on coastal excursions; the 'rocket' is 63 ft long, carries 140 passengers and is reputedly the fastest excursion boat in the world.

Palm Beach Pop. 110,000
Palm Beach island is the millionaires' playground. Supposedly 70% of the world's richest people are permanently resident or at least own a home here. The island is 13 miles long and about half a mile wide and faces the mainland city of *West Palm Beach* (pop. 57,000). They are linked by three bridges. Palm Beach is ideal for a relaxing holiday; giant palms fringe the streets, and elegant villas stand in beautifully maintained parks. Adequate funds are a prerequisite if you choose to holiday in Palm Beach as the resort is very expensive.

 What to see
The railroad pioneer Henry Flagler built his superb villa *Whitehall* in 1901. Today it houses the *Flagler Museum*, including among the exhibits Flagler's own luxury railway carriage. In West Palm Beach the *Norton Gallery of Art* (1451 S Oliver Avenue) is worth a visit. The gallery includes a large collection of French paintings, contemporary American art, and Chinese jade and ceramics. Art objects are also on display at the modern *Esplanade* shopping centre, where the rich may be admired in the *Café*

Melbourne Beach

l'Europe. *The Breakers* (1 South County Road) is a particularly sophisticated establishment and the oldest luxury hotel in Florida, where guests often arrive in Bentleys and Rolls Royces.

A beach of fine sand lined with palm trees, but unfortunately closed to the public in many places.

Window-shopping in romantic *Worth Avenue* with its exclusive boutiques should be included on any visit to Palm Beach. The creations of the world's top fashion designers are sold here.

Petite Marmite (French/Italian cuisine) on Worth Avenue is one of the most renowned gourmet restaurants in the USA. Less elegant, but with a more congenial atmosphere, is *Peter Dinkel's* on Royal Poinciana Way, a restaurant with garden and sidewalk café.

Direct air links with many US cities from Palm Beach International Airport.

Ex Drive west on Southern Boulevard to reach *Lion Country Safari*, a park where lions, elephants, bison and antelopes roam free in the grounds.

Melbourne Beach Pop. 2,300

This small beach resort on an island opposite the industrial town of *Melbourne* (pop. 42,000) is of particular interest to surfers and also to amateur zoologists. The strong breakers on Melbourne Beach create ideal conditions for surfing.

Quiet sandy beach, but not very suitable for bathing because of high surf.

A special tip

In midsummer marine turtles may be observed at night as they lay their eggs in the sand on secluded parts of the beach. The turtles hatch in September and October.

Cocoa Beach Pop. 13,000

NASA personnel from the *Kennedy Space Center* and military personnel from the *Cape Canaveral* air-force base spend their leisure time here. The town caters for many sporting and entertainment activities. Cocoa Beach is primarily of interest to divers. A number of Spanish galleons sank off the coast of *Brevard County* and treasure chests and other valuables are still being brought to the surface. Cocoa Beach and its 330-yd-long wooden jetty are perfect for surf fishing. This is the place to catch the big fish from dry land if the cost of chartering a boat in Florida seems too high.

 Extensive white sandy beaches.

 Amateur divers are not permitted to treasure-hunt on sunken ships.

Titusville Pop. 30,500

The town is situated only 2 miles from the *Kennedy Space Center*, but can offer all kinds of holiday activities besides this unique attraction.

Kennedy Space Center

The John F. Kennedy Space Center on *Cape Canaveral* lies close to the *Merritt Island National Wildlife Refuge*, a conservation area for endangered species of birds. On Sundays visitors may wander round the Spaceport but it is better to take the NASA guided bus tours which allow greater access to the complex.

 Man's greatest adventure began at Cape Canaveral. On July 16th 1969 the American astronauts Neil

Kennedy Space Center

Launching Atlanta *from Cape Canaveral*

Armstrong, Edwin Aldrin and Michael Collins took off on the first manned mission to the moon. On July 21st Commander Neil Armstrong was the first man to set foot on the moon; he was joined shortly afterwards by Edwin Aldrin from the lunar module, while Michael Collins orbited the moon in the *Apollo 11* space capsule.

On April 12th 1981 the Space Shuttle *Columbia* was launched for the first time, introducing a new era of manned space flights. The enterprise suffered a severe set-back when the Space Shuttle *Challenger* exploded on January 28th 1986 shortly after take-off, killing seven astronauts.

It all began on July 24th 1950 when a V2 rocket, developed by Dr Wernher von Braun, was launched at Cape Canaveral and heralded the beginning of NASA (National Aeronautics and Space Administration). On May 5th 1961 Alan Shephard took off on a 114-mile journey into space. On February 20th 1962 John Glenn was the first American to orbit the Earth in a space capsule.

 What to see

A visit to the Kennedy Space Center begins at the *Visitors Center* which can be reached via Cocoa Beach or Titusville. Admission is free and conducted tours are held continuously throughout the day. The *Hall of History* provides a good insight into the history of space exploration. The film *The Dream is Alive*, shown on the giant screen of the *IMAX Theater*, will definitely set the mood for your visit, and there are exhibitions on space travel in the *Galaxy Theater* and *Theater One*. Outside the building, the *Rocket Garden* contains various carrier rockets.

Tickets for the 2-hour bus tour through the space centre are available at the Visitors Center. The route passes a number of launch sites on the way to the centre of the Spaceport. Alligators may be seen along the route as large areas of the site belong to the Merritt Island wildlife park. The tour continues to the *Industrial Area* where rockets and space vehicles are manufactured. In the astronaut training centre you can get an impression of the severe trials endured

Daytona Beach

by the American astronauts. *Apollo 11* was launched to the moon from the *Complex 39 Launch Control Center*. An *Air Force Space Museum* can also be seen.

i A timetable of rocket launches is given on freephone (800) 432 2153; at present there are only occasional test flights. Further information from *NASA Tours Division, Visitors Center*.

Ex The wildlife conservation area *Canaveral National Seashore* lies south of the space centre and is rich in fauna and shells. The sand-dune beaches at *Playalinda* and *Apollo* are designated bathing areas. A pathway leads to *Turtle Mound*, a hill of shells created by Indians in the 14th c.

✈ *Cape Kennedy Regional Airport* at Melbourne is used by many airlines.

Daytona Beach Pop. 65,000

The resort at Daytona Beach is mainly favoured by families with children as many big attractions such as Disney World and the Kennedy Space Center are within easy reach. Daytona Beach candidly refers to itself as 'The World's Most Famous Beach'. You can drive a car along the 23-mile-long firm sand beach, which in places is some hundred yards wide. There is a long tradition of motor racing in Daytona and in neighbouring *Ormond Beach*. In 1902 the first race took place on the beach; nowadays the races are held on the *Daytona International Speedway*. In particular, the Daytona Auto Racing in February attracts racing fans from all over the world. The circuit can be visited by bus except on racing days. Tourists should try to avoid the town if possible during Daytona Beach's second annual invasion at the beginning of March, when college students on spring vacation arrive in force to soak up the sun. Up to half a million students take over the hotels for a period of three to four weeks.

 The Museum of Arts and Sciences (1040 Museum Boulevard) has a collection of Cuban art, and a department of natural history with a giant saurian skeleton. The well-known *Museum of Speed* in Ormond Beach (79 E Granada Avenue) exhibits past and modern speed-record-holding racing cars.

 The widest and longest beach in Florida, in places with high sand dunes. There is an excellent view of the beach from the Space Needle boardwalk.

The big motor races take place in February and July, with motorcycle racing in March and October. There is greyhound racing near the circuit at the *Kennel Club*, and also *Jai alai*.

 Bicycle and motorcycle hire.

Numerous discotheques and nightclubs. Rock and disco music predominates for the young majority. There are concerts of classical and pop music in the *Peabody Auditorium*. At the end of August there is a large Spanish fiesta. Beach concerts in summer.

Try the *Pump House East Restaurant* if you like something out of the ordinary. The restaurant is built entirely of weather-worn wood and decorated with display cases of antique dolls, cradles and other objects from the pioneering days of the USA. A particular speciality of the house is fish baked in parchment.

The Daytona Beach Municipal Airport has services to and from various cities in the USA on several American airlines.

 Boat trips on the *Seabreeze Yacht II* from South Memorial Bridge to *Ponce de León Inlet* and other neighbouring islands.

 Marineland of Florida, 31 miles to the north. An extensive complex housing about 1,000 different marine animals. The dolphin displays and the sharks feeding underwater are particularly interesting. Open daily 8 am to 6 pm.

Saint Augustine Pop. 13,000

Over 400 years old, St Augustine is the oldest town in the USA and many historic buildings from the Spanish period are still to be seen. The Old Town has retained much of its original charm with narrow pedestrian streets adorned with flowers, and small shops, pleasant restaurants and wine taverns. Those visitors who prefer not to walk can be driven through the old quarter by (horse-drawn) coach. St Augustine also has good beaches and a variety of sporting and entertainment facilities.

On September 8th 1565 the Spaniard Pedro Menéndez de Avilés founded St Augustine as the headquarters of his campaign against the French, who had built *Fort Caroline* a year earlier on the present-day site of *Jacksonville*. Menéndez took the fort and slaughtered its troops on the island of Anastasia, 13 miles south of St Augustine. Between 1565 and 1675 the Spanish constructed nine wooden forts to protect the fast-growing town, and in 1672 work started on the construction of the massive stone fortress *Castillo de San Marcos*. Between 1763 and 1784 St

The Lightner Museum, St Augustine

Augustine was in English hands; the Spanish then took over again until 1819. Then the Americans arrived, and at the end of the 19th c. Flagler, the oil millionaire, began converting the sleepy township into a winter retreat for wealthy northerners.

 What to see

St Augustine is best seen from the *Sightseeing Train* which stops at all the important historical sites on its 7-mile tour of the town.

Opposite the *Plaza de la Constitución*, the Spanish commercial quarter, stands the *Cathedral of St Augustine*, one of the oldest churches in the USA. The old town centre, *San Agustín Antiguo*, has been gradually restored, together with the town wall, over the last decades. *George Street* and the narrow neighbouring streets are lined with handsome 16th and 17th c. Spanish residences. Many of the houses have been equipped with period furnishings. Today several serve as museums, and others have been reconstructed as old craft workshops, general stores (Oldest Store) and a Spanish inn (*Mesa Sanchez*), with attendants dressed in 19th c. costume.

The *Castillo de San Marcos* is very impressive; it is the oldest stone fortress in the USA and offers a magnificent view over Matanzas Bay. Other interesting sights include *Zorayda Castle*, modelled on the Alhambra, housing a major art collection; the *Alcazar Hotel* built by Flagler, which today houses the town hall and the *Lightner Museum* with a collection of Tiffany-style glass; *Potter's Wax Museum* containing over 240 figures; *Yesterday's Toys* museum in the *Rodriguez Avera House*, with valuable puppets from the Milan Opera; and *Ripley's Believe It Or Not Museum* with curiosities from all over the world. The *World's Original Alligator Attraction* stages hourly 'battles' between man and alligator from 9 am for sensation-seeking onlookers.

 White sandy beaches with dunes in St Augustine Beach and Vilano Beach.

 Many small antique-shops in the Old Town.

 Major events almost throughout the year: a jazz festival in March, an arts and crafts fair in April and 'Spanish Week' in August.

 Ocean Grove on Highway A1A with all facilities, and other campsites in the surrounding area.

Jacksonville Pop. 590,000

The metropolis on the St Johns River occupies the largest area of any city in the western world: its boundaries encompass 840 sq miles. Jacksonville is an important naval base and a centre of the armaments industry. The inner city is a modern commercial centre which boasts Florida's tallest skyscraper (530 ft). It is interesting to wander around *Jacksonville Port*, one of the busiest on the south-east coast and full of atmosphere.

 What to see

Sights worth seeing include *Fort Caroline National Memorial*, a reconstruction of the fort erected by the French in 1564; *Kingsley Plantation* on *Fort George Island*, at one time a centre of the slave trade, with the masters' houses, slave quarters and a museum; *Jacksonville Museum of Arts and Sciences* with a planetarium and 'cosmic concerts'; *Cummer Gallery of Art*, with precious Oriental and Meissen porcelain; and *Jacksonville Children's Museum. Friendship Fountain* also deserves a souvenir snapshot with its 114-ft-high jets of water. *Jacksonville Zoo* is on Trout River and contains exotic animals. A few miles to the north of the city there is a good beach and camping facilities at *Little Talbot Island State Park*. The beach is quieter than Jacksonville Beach. Paddle-steamer trips on the St Johns River.

 Good white sandy beach at Jacksonville Beach.

 Several large shopping centres.

 Occasional guest performances by orchestras and theatre companies. Two local ballet ensembles.

 American football at *Gator Bowl*, basketball tournaments in the *Coliseum*, greyhound racing at *Orange Park*. There are comprehensive sports facilities within the city, but often great distances separate the individual sports centres. All watersports amenities are available at *Jacksonville Beach*.

 Jacksonville Landing will tempt shoppers; a stroll on *River Walk* along the St Johns River is more relaxing.

 Large city festival in September.

 Several sites in the city area.

 Jacksonville International Airport with services to many US cities.

Sunbathing on the west coast

The west coast

The resorts are situated on the 155 miles or so of coastline between *Marco Island* and *Clearwater*. The area north of Clearwater has hardly been developed for tourism and therefore none of its towns have been mentioned here. As yet there are not as many visitors to the west coast as to the east coast. Resorts such as Marco Island or *Captiva* are still regarded almost as insider tips for the peaceful enjoyment of Florida's beauty.

St Petersburg and Clearwater offer more sport and entertainment facilities but also bigger crowds. From December to February the average temperature of 63°F/17°C makes it a little chilly for bathing. This tour however begins in the tropical south.

Marco Island

Marco Island first revealed its holiday paradise potential in the 1970s and soon the exclusive resort became the favourite second home of wealthy Americans. It also has elegant hotels and an array of sport and entertainment facilities to offer, and even its own little airline. For a long time environmentalists and investors battled over the development of the island for tourism. The construction industry won in the end, but the hotels and apartment buildings erected here tend to be smaller than elsewhere and there are no concrete 'monstrosities' on Marco Island.

 Sandy beaches, where a great number of beautiful shells may be found.

 The *Ten Thousand Islands* area is famous for its excellent fishing grounds. It is perfect for deep-sea fishing enthusiasts.

 The *Marco Beach and Villas* hotel complex has superb sports facilities.

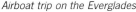 Marco Island Airways offers a service to and from Miami.

Naples Pop. 21,000

The gateway to the Everglades is linked to the east coast by a highway and is a pleasant resort with avenues of palm trees and well-maintained parks. The town has been called the Palm Beach of the west coast because of its many luxury villas. In contrast to the millionaires' paradise, Naples does provide more for the average tourist with a range of inexpensive motels as well as the luxury-class accommodation. In addition, the beach is freely accessible to the public everywhere. Anglers once more crowd on to the 330-yd-long pier, the prize possession of Naples, following its reconstruction (the pier was destroyed in a hurricane in 1964).

Visit Jane Tetzlaff's *African Safari Park* in *Caribbean Gardens*, a wildlife park in a tropical setting at the edge of the Everglades. Big cats such as lions, tigers, pumas, leopards and tiglons (a cross between tiger and lion) can be seen. There are excursions in the open-top

Airboat trip on the Everglades

Bonita Beach near Naples

Safari Train and also walking tours on special routes.

 Miles of sandy beaches, with access roads and free parking at regular intervals. Also a good place for shell-collectors.

 Naples Depot is a curiosity: the depot has been renovated and its railway carriages contain shops. There are also plenty of small shops housed in picturesque old buildings. The best shopping areas are *Old Naples* on *Third Street South* and the *Old Marine Market Place*.

 Wooten's Airboat Tours in Ochopee offer trips through the Everglades.

✈ *PBA/Naples Airlines* run a regular daily service between *Naples Municipal Airport* and Miami and Tampa.

Ex Over 100 years ago *Big Cypress Swamp* on the outskirts of Naples was the refuge of the last surviving Seminole Indians; today their descendants live on the reservation here. From the boardwalk crossing *Corkscrew Swamp* you can see giant ferns, rare orchids, alligators and 700-year-old cypresses.

Fort Myers/Fort Myers Beach
Pop. 44,000

The elegant charm of Fort Myers, also known as the 'City of Palms' on account of its many palm-lined boulevards, is a legacy of the turn of the century. The 15-mile-long McGregor Boulevard is considered the most picturesque of the palm avenues. Fort Myers Beach, situated on a string of offshore islands, offers all amenities for a relaxing holiday. The area on either side of Fort Myers, including the nearby islands of *Sanibel*, *Captiva* and *Pine Island*, is known as the *Lee Island Coast*.

📷 *Thomas A. Edison's Winter Home*. Edison (1847–1931), the inventor of the electric lightbulb, had to move to Florida from Maine when he was thirty-nine, for health reasons. His house (with a botanical garden) on McGregor Boulevard has remained unaltered since his time and now serves as a museum. The *natural history museum* will interest children. 3½ miles north of Fort Myers is the *Shell Factory* with a collection of rare shells and coral from all over the world. Souvenirs on sale.

 Good sandy beach at Fort Myers Beach.

 Fort Myers Beach and around the Lee Island Coast area.

 Musicals and concerts at the *Lee County Arena* (North Fort Myers).

 Several flights daily to many US cities from *Fort Myers Southwest Florida Regional Airport*.

Edison's house, Fort Myers

Trips on the *Caloosahatchee River* through unspoilt jungle. At Bonita Springs, 18 miles to the south, you can visit the *Everglades Wonder Gardens*, a wildlife park in the swamps with alligators, otters, bears and panthers.

Sanibel and Captiva

Both these islands off Fort Myers are dream resorts. The romantic jungle wilderness has remained intact despite the quantity of good hotels and motels here. Alligators still roam wild on Sanibel and Captiva, which are linked by a small bridge. The wide sandy beaches, a paradise for shell-seekers, are certainly among the finest in Florida. The islands can be reached from Fort Myers via a toll bridge. All types of sports facilities are available. As on Marco Island, the islanders once fought a bitter battle against mass tourism. Their main aim was to prevent the construction of the bridge to the mainland, but they failed. However, this hardly created any problems, since the two nature conservation areas (recommended) that were the primary concern of the environmentalists have not proved as popular as the glorious beaches. And the much-feared 'concrete jungle' architecture never appeared on either Sanibel or Captiva.

The main attraction is the *J. N. Darling National Wildlife Refuge*, a mangrove wilderness of 7 sq miles, with alligators, raccoons, otters, and brown pelicans with 6-ft wing-spans. The wildlife area may be explored on foot (route maps available at the entrance), on guided tours and via canoe expeditions. The lighthouse, built in 1884, is a trademark of Sanibel. On the nearby beaches, giant loggerhead turtles may be seen laying their eggs in summer.

Public beach on Sanibel Island

 Miles of wide sandy beaches where it is easy to find a secluded spot.

 Many hotels include the use of rowing boats, sailing craft or motorboats in their prices.

 No need to put to sea for a prize catch. There is excellent fishing from the *Sanibel-Captiva Fishing Pier*.

 In the *South Seas Plantation* holiday complex.

 The small shops on *Periwinkle Way* on Sanibel sell souvenirs and shell jewellery.

 Sanibel is ideal for exploring by bicycle. Cycle hire from Periwinkle Way.

 Some small, pleasant restaurants serving seafood specialities.

 Sanibel hosts the *Shell Fair* on the first weekend in March, attracting visitors from all over Florida.

Sarasota Pop. 51,000

The town extends over 19 sq miles and has well-maintained gardens and parks, good shopping areas and high-quality beaches within its limits. Many artists and writers have settled here. Sarasota is also the home of the world-famous circus Ringling Bros., Barnum & Bailey. Mr Ringling made his fortune in oil, property and railroad construction. His millions were invested in the 'Greatest Show on Earth' where they multiplied nicely. One of Sarasota's grandest boulevards bears his name. His own legacy to the town is an art museum and a circus museum at *Ca'd'Zan*, his mansion, and the *Asolo Theater*.

 What to see

Almost everything revolves around the circus in Sarasota. In the *Circus Hall of Fame* museum there are puppet shows and magic tricks on display. Circus performances are held in June, July and August. John Ringling's luxury villa, which was modelled on the Doge's Palace in Venice, belongs to the group of *Ringling Museums*. It contains an art museum, with one of the world's largest collections of works by Rubens, and an exhibition tracing the history of the circus. Visitors who are keen on model railways will enjoy the *Lionel Train and Seashell Museum* near the airport. *Bellm's Museum of Cars and Music of Yesterday* has a display of classic cars and musical boxes. Alligators, monkeys, flamingos and parrots live in the *Sarasota Jungle Gardens*.

 Extensive fine sandy beaches within the town limits.

 Elegant boutiques in the town centre.

 Concerts and classical theatre productions in the *Asolo Theater*, a faithfully reconstructed 18th c. Italian theatre.

 Sarasota Airport has daily direct flights within Florida and to some US cities.

 Excursions by Mississippi paddle-steamer from *Marina Jack*.

Venice (south of Sarasota) is the winter quarters of the Ringling Brothers Circus, with the *Ringling Clown College* where visitors can watch artistes train. The wildlife preserve *Myakka River State Park* east of Sarasota will interest nature-lovers (bicycle hire).

Bradenton Pop. 28,000

This town situated at the mouth of the *Manatee River* is not an obvious tourist choice but has a number of interesting sights. It is worth a stopover if you are travelling from Sarasota to St Petersburg.

 What to see

The *DeSoto National Memorial* stands at the mouth of the Manatee River. The

Flamingos in the Sarasota Jungle Gardens

Replica of the Bounty, *St Petersburg*

Spaniard Hernando de Soto landed on Florida's west coast in 1539 and made his way up to the Mississippi River. A film traces the history of the expedition. The *South Florida Museum and Bishop Planetarium* provides a good survey of Florida's history from the Stone Age to the Space Age. A canoeing trip on the Manatee River will require more energy as it takes up to five hours to complete the five-mile route. The Manatee is named after the sea-cow which is native to the river.

 Lake Manatee Recreation Area.

Longboat Key and Ana Maria Island

The two elongated islands off Bradenton with the townships of *Longboat Key, Bradenton Beach, Holmes Beach* and *Ana Maria* offer a complete range of leisure facilities. Scenically they are not in the same class as Sanibel and Captiva.

Extensive wide sandy beaches.

 Fresh stone-crab and fish specialities at *Moore's Stone Crab* waterfront restaurant in Longboat Key. The restaurant has its own tame dolphin.

St Petersburg Pop. 240,000

Situated on Tampa Bay and the Gulf of Mexico, the city of St Petersburg is surrounded on three sides by water. The offshore bathing resorts of *Treasure Island, St Petersburg Beach* and *Redington* have made St Petersburg popular both as a holiday centre and as a retirement area for affluent senior citizens.

Williams Park in the heart of the city is the venue of frequent open-air concerts. Nearby on the waterfront with its own harbour in *Demens Landing Park* is 'The Pier', a five-storey inverted pyramid with a restaurant, shops and observation terrace. In 1885 the city was declared a climatic health resort by the American

Sunset, St Petersburg

Sunken Gardens, St Petersburg

Medical Association, and even today the air purity in the inner city ranks St Petersburg among the ten cleanest cities of the USA.

 What to see

Sunken Gardens
(1825 4th Street North): The Sunken Gardens contain over 7,000 species of tropical flowers and plants, and 50,000 flowering annuals are freshly planted every year. There are camellias, azaleas and rhododendrons in abundance.

Salvador Dali Museum
(1000 3rd Street South): A. Reynolds Morse, a wealthy engineering-factory owner from Ohio, spent forty years compiling this collection of 93 oil paintings, 200 watercolours and drawings, and over 1,000 other works by the Spanish Surrealist. The collection has been valued at between 50 and 70 million dollars.

St Petersburg Historical Museum
(3350th block on 2nd Avenue): Exhibitions of Indian culture and natural history.

Fort Desoto Park
A conservation area of 985 acres with 7 miles of beaches, it is one of the loveliest recreation parks in the country. Situated around the abandoned fort, the park lies to the south of the city on *Mullet Key* and affords a good view of ships passing into and out of St Petersburg.

Bayfront Center
(400 1st Street South): Venue for pop and rock concerts, Broadway shows and circus performances.

Kopsick Palm Arboretum
(225 Beach Drive): Over 200 palms and 45 different varieties on display.

Coliseum Ballroom
(535 4th Avenue North): This famous building with its enormous palais de danse was opened in 1924 and has served as a backdrop in various films. Nowadays the ballroom hosts concerts by well-known Big Bands; open Wednesdays 8 pm to 11 pm and Saturdays 9 pm to 1 am.

 Miles of sandy beaches on the offshore islands.

In St Petersburg there is almost every kind of spectator sport: international golf and tennis tournaments, dog- and horse-racing, basketball, baseball, motorboat racing and the fastest sea-plane race in the world (usually held in February). There is even ice hockey in the *Bayfront Center*. All types of watersports are available in St Petersburg Beach, Treasure Island and Redington.

  Tennis and golf facilities also on the beaches.

Countryside Mall, Clearwater

Several in the surrounding area.

Direct air links with major US cities from *St Petersburg Clearwater International Airport*; some international services, mainly to the Caribbean.

Clearwater Pop. 82,000
Clearwater harbour is the base of the largest sports fishing fleet in Florida. The town is situated on a hill on the Pinellas peninsula overlooking the Gulf of Mexico. It is quieter and a little more exclusive here than in St Petersburg 21 miles away.

 What to see

Boatyard Village
(16100 Fairchild Drive): A reconstruction of a 19th c. New England fishing village with historic wooden houses, shops and daily shows.

Clearwater Beach

Moccasin Lake Nature Park
(2759 Park Trail Lane): A 60-acre nature park with a lake, forest and indigenous flora and fauna. Closed on Mondays.

Marine Science Center
(249 Windward Passage): A place to study the marine life in the Gulf of Mexico. Research centre and sanctuary for aquatic wildlife.

4-mile white sandy beach on *Clearwater Beach* island; parts are closed to the public. *Caladesi Island State Park* where vehicles are prohibited is a good tip for a quiet swim or a stroll along the trails through the tropical parkland. Access by ferry from *Dunedin*.

Ex To *Homosassa Springs*, about 62 miles to the north. Large recreation park with alligators, otters, hippos and even kangaroos. The biggest attraction is the enormous *Fish Bowl* where visitors can watch over 1,000 different

fish swim around them from inside a glass dome. The *Weeki Wachee Attractions* are situated between Clearwater and Homosassa, and consist of an underwater theatre, river trips and bird displays.

People still dive for sponges in *Tarpon Springs*, once a Greek settlement. The *St Nicholas Greek Orthodox Cathedral* in North Pinellas Avenue was inspired by the church of Hagia Sophia in Istanbul. You could be forgiven for thinking you were in Greece on Dodecanese Boulevard.

Tampa Pop. 280,000
Three bridges spanning Tampa Bay connect Florida's third largest city with St Petersburg and Clearwater. Tampa, the fastest growing industrial centre in the state, is the seventh biggest commercial port in the USA. Cruise ships to Mexico and the Caribbean also depart from here. The Cuban quarter *Ybor City*, formerly a centre of cigar production, is situated on Hillsborough Bay.

The Trade Center, Tampa

Top: The university. Above: Busch Gardens, Tampa

 What to see

Tampa's most interesting feature is the *Busch Gardens* African theme park. There are extensive grounds with over 350 animal species, including rhinos, elephants, camels, lions and zebras; a Moroccan palace with a theatre; the *Nairobi* animal nursery; *Stanleyville* African village; the *Timbuktu* bazaar; belly-dancers; and rides on the rapids. *Tampa Museum* (601 Doyle Carlton Road) houses temporary art and historical exhibitions. The renovated *Ybor City* quarter has retained much of its Cuban atmosphere: there are narrow streets, colonial-style houses with wrought-iron balconies and painted tiles, typical restaurants and sidewalk cafés. The old cigar factory on *Ybor Square* has been converted to house boutiques and theatres. Hand-rolled cigars may be bought at the *Nostalgia Market* and fresh coffee in the *Navier Coffee Mill.* The *Ybor City State Museum* (1818 9th Avenue) traces the history of the cigar industry.

Water-lovers will enjoy *Aquamania* (2001 East Fowler Avenue) which includes four 390-ft-long curving water-chutes. A little further on, children may stroke the animals at the zoo in *Lowry Park*, and there are life-sized fairy-tale figures at the *Fairyland Park and Zoo*.

 Campsite with all facilities at Busch Gardens.

Services to many major US cities, to the Caribbean and Mexico from *Tampa International Airport.*

Epcot Center, Orlando

Central Florida

Central Florida is the location of the world-famous tourist attraction Walt Disney World, near Orlando. Every year this land of make-believe draws millions of visitors from all over the world. Outside the USA, the rest of central Florida is hardly acknowledged as a tourist area. The gentle rolling hills are dotted with stud farms, enormous citrus plantations, large and small lakes, and rivers. The area is ideal for fishing and for boating holidays on the St Johns River between Orlando and Jacksonville.

Most tourists only associate central Florida with an excursion to Disney World and consequently the following holiday centres are dealt with briefly. However, you may even be tempted to spend your holiday in Florida's lakelands. The weather here is mild throughout the year: in winter the temperatures rarely fall below 60°F/15°C, and in summer they hardly ever exceed 81°F/27°C.

Lake Okeechobee

Lake Okeechobee covering an area of 730 sq miles is the largest inland sea in the USA after Lake Michigan. The very calm waters are a paradise for birds, and hundreds of species nest here. The towns on the lake offer good holiday facilities, particularly for anglers, and around the lake there are a number of sights worthy of at least a brief visit.

Okeechobee Pop. 4,000

The town is situated on the northern end of the lake and is a centre for the cattle and dairy industries. Here you can attend big cattle-auctions or visit the rodeos.

 Okee-Tantie Recreation Area south of the town, cabin cruisers may be hired to sail on the lake or the Kissimmee River.

△ *Crystal Lakes Resort* on US 441, with full facilities including swimming pool, golf course and tennis courts.

Ex *Brighton Seminole Indian Reservation* on the west shore of the lake, where Indian artefacts are sold. Rodeo in August.

Sebring is famous for its motor racing; the 12-hour race in March attracts many thousands of spectators.

Lake Wales Pop. 8,500

The township is surrounded by lakes and citrus plantations. It is a peaceful holiday centre for anglers and riders. The *Lake Kissimmee* recreation park offers 495 acres for hiking, swimming, fishing and sailing. In *Masterpiece Gardens* there is a large mosaic of Leonardo da Vinci's famous painting *The Last Supper* measuring 12 ft by 24 ft, and consisting of over 300,000 coloured stones. The *Singing Tower*, famous for its 53-bell chimes, is 295 ft high and made of pink marble and shell limestone. The full 45-minute chime may be heard daily at 3 pm, with shorter versions every half hour.

A special tip

The *Black Hills Passion Play* at Lake Wales is spectacular. It involves over 700 participants and is performed regularly in spring (February to April).

Water Ski Revue, Cypress Gardens

Cypress Gardens

Chalet Suzanne, a restaurant in a castle, offers unusual international specialities. Try the dessert of baked grapefruit halves with sugar and cinnamon.

Cypress Gardens

The veteran of recreation parks, *Cypress Gardens* lies on the shores of Lake Eloise near the sleepy little town of *Winter Haven*.

The imaginative real-estate dealer Dick Pope created the 160-acre tropical gardens in 1936. Thousands of varieties of flowers and plants grow here among cypresses hundreds of years old, and grottos, ponds and pathways. Visitors can stroll through the park or take an electric boat on the numerous canals. The *Water Ski Revue* is a highlight and a show of spectacular artistry. Performances at 10 am, noon, 2 pm and 4 pm. The *Island in the Sky* allows you a bird's-eye view of the park.

Winter Haven

There is a detailed survey of citrus-fruit cultivation in the *Citrus Showcase*, an exhibition promoted by local plantation-owners. Antique dolls, toys and miniatures from over the centuries can be seen at the *Museum of Old Dolls and Toys*.

 Several in the surrounding area.

 To the north-west stands the large *Lakeland College* complex where many buildings were designed by the famous architect Frank Lloyd Wright.

Kissimmee Pop. 13,000

The first bars were opened in Kissimmee in 1870, and at that time they were all 'open-air' to accommodate the cowboys as they quenched their thirst on horseback. Nowadays there are still real cowboys around as Kissimmee is a centre for cattle breeding. Catering for nearby Disney World, the town offers excellent overnight accommodation, ranging from basic hotels to luxury-class establishments, and good sporting and entertainment facilities.

 Indian World Museum with a collection of Indian artefacts. *Gatorland Zoo*, the largest alligator farm in Florida, where visitors may also feed crocodiles, is situated in the north of the town. To the west are *Water Mania*, an extensive water playground and picnic park with Florida's largest wave pool, and *Medieval Times*, where guests can dine at a medieval tournament in the setting of an old castle.

 Makinson's Store sells reasonably priced cowboy boots, hand-tooled saddles, spurs and lassoos.

 The large *Silver Spurs Rodeo* at the end of February and the beginning of July. Book your hotel accommodation in Kissimmee in advance if you plan to visit at these times.

Orlando Pop. 130,000

The town is the gateway to Walt Disney World and other amusement parks. Orlando used to be a quiet backwater whose inhabitants made their living chiefly from the surrounding orange-plantations. It all changed in 1971 when Mickey Mouse arrived on the scene. Within two years, the number of hotel beds rose astronomically, from 4,000 to 60,000. Today the town lives almost exclusively from tourism.

 What to see

Stars Hall of Fame (6825 Starway Drive), a wax museum with over 200 figures of famous actors and singers, is worth a visit. The *Elvis Presley Museum* (5931 American Way) is a must for rock-and-roll fans. *Loch Haven Art Center* displays 20th c. American art. Within the greater Orlando area there are forty-seven parks and fifty-four lakes, the most impressive of these being Lake Eola.

Bars with all types of music, and discos, in the *Church Street Station* district.

Trotting races in *Casselberry* (May to September), greyhound racing at *Longwood* and *Jai alai* in Fern Park. Riding and tennis tournaments during the *Orlando Horse Show*.

Resort Mission Inn.

The *Wet 'n Wild* water amusement park (6200 International Drive) will refresh water-lovers.

Sea World, Orlando

Closing firework display, Sea World

✈ Orlando International Airport has services to and from most major US cities. Eastern Airlines is the 'official' Disney World airline and offers good package deals.

Ex The major amusement parks (such as Disney World and Sea World) have separate entries. A number of tour companies offer bus excursions to these attractions.

Sea World

The 300-acre marine theme park, one of the best in the world, is situated on Interstate 4 between Orlando and Walt Disney World. At least half a day is necessary to see all the attractions here (open daily 9 am to 8 pm). The best-known star of the marine animal ensemble is Shamu the killer whale. There are unique shows with dolphins, sea-lions,

Sea World, Orlando

seals, sharks, penguins and otters. In the *Atlantis Theater*, which can accommodate 5,000 spectators, the motto is 'almost anything goes' (on water, that is). Speed-boat pilots carry out hair-raising stunts, magicians perform their tricks on water-skis, and scenes from popular TV series are re-enacted on water. There are computer-operated fountains, a tidal pool, penguins in realistic polar surroundings, Japanese pearl-divers and a 125,000-gallon seawater aquarium. Visitors can feed the dolphins and seals – an unforgettable experience for children. There is also a huge playground for children to enjoy. You can see half of Florida from the viewing tower, which is over 300 ft high.

Over 10,000 hotel rooms nearby; most hotels offer their guests a free commuter bus service.

Boardwalk and Baseball
Circus World, which had been an attrac-tion for many years, was replaced in 1987 by the *Boardwalk and Baseball* amusement park. There are roller coaster rides, and all the information baseball fanatics could want about their favourite sport. Open daily 9 am to 10 pm, at weekends to midnight.

Walt Disney World
The 43 sq miles of the Walt Disney World resort are situated on Interstate 4 some 18 miles south-west of Orlando. Walt Disney World is Florida's most famous attraction and draws millions of visitors every year. Wherever you happen to be in Florida, there are bound to be excursion trips by bus or plane to this mammoth amusement park. If possible allow three days for your visit; it is worth buying a multiple-visit ticket, available in the resort hotels or in the *Transportation and Ticket Center*, which is valid for all amusements.

Walt Disney World is made up of the *Magic Kingdom* and *Epcot Center*

Walt Disney World. Left: Disney-MGM Studios. Right: Typhoon Lagoon

Main Street USA, Walt Disney World

which was opened in 1982. New attractions have been added since 1989. The *Disney-MGM Studios* theme park shows how films are produced. *Typhoon Lagoon* is a water theme park with a wave pool, giant water-chutes and waterfalls. In the evening, *Pleasure Island* offers restaurants and lively nightclubs. The Magic Kingdom is divided into six sections, Epcot Center into two.

Magic Kingdom
(Open 9 am to midnight in summer, till 7 pm in winter.)

Main Street USA. As you go through the main gates you enter a small American town of the turn of the century, with picturesque house façades. Main Street USA leads to the fairy-tale castle around which the other sections are grouped. Walt Disney's films are shown at the *Main Street Cinema*. The street is lined with shops and restaurants. The double-decker sightseeing buses, horse-drawn carriages and train tours around the Magic Kingdom set off from here.

Adventureland proves just how realistic a make-believe world can appear with its computer-operated figures in a true-to-life setting. On a boat trip through the jungle you could believe you were surrounded by real elephants, tigers, hippos, snakes and tropical singing birds; the Pirates of the Caribbean also get up to all kinds of escapades.

Frontierland is devoted to a Wild West

Walt Disney World

theme, with a shooting arcade, Western saloon and Country music. The *Big Thunder Mountain Railroad* leads to a gold-mining town. Realistic earthquakes and avalanches are simulated.

Liberty Square is the place to board the Mississippi paddle-steamer. In a hall, the figures of forty US Presidents, from Lincoln to Reagan, not only move but speak as well.

Fantasyland brings the stars of Walt Disney's films to life. Here you can meet Mickey Mouse, accompany Captain Nemo on the Nautilus '20,000 leagues under the sea', see Dumbo the flying elephant or visit *Cinderella's Castle*.

World of Motion, Future World

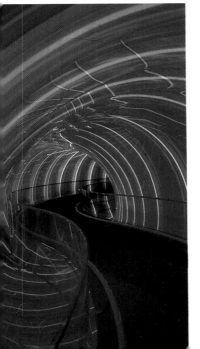

Tomorrowland. In the world of the future the Space Mountain roller coaster plunges through darkness at breathtaking speed, and a giant spaceship heads for Mars accompanied by original NASA film of the 'red planet'. A balloon trip reveals the USA's most impressive sights by means of a circular cinema.

Epcot Center
(Open daily 9 am to 10 pm in summer, till 9 pm in winter.)

Future World. *Spaceship Earth* is the spherical symbol of tomorrow's world, with a fascinating portrayal of human communication from Stone Age cave paintings to satellite technology. In *Communicore* applied earth-bound technology is demonstrated, from the most up-to-date travel information to the future communication of news. Visitors to the *Universe of Energy* are transported through time by means of solar energy from the beginning of the Earth's geological development up to the energy sources of this century. *Horizons* highlights lifestyles in the 21st century. *The World of Motion* depicts the development of transportation; *Journey into Imagination* reveals the world of dreams with the aid of ultra-modern technology. *The Land* offers an informative and enjoyable insight into agriculture and nutrition. *The Living Seas*, the largest marine aquarium in the world, allows a close encounter from within its acrylic-walled tunnel with over 200 species of marine fauna – over 6,000 creatures in all. Visitors glide through the water in glass gondolas to *Seabase Alpha*, the model of an underwater research station.

The new Wonders of Life Pavilion includes Body Wars, a flight-simulator ride through the human body.

World Showcase is the second theme area in Epcot Center. Eleven nations

Parade, Walt Disney World

display their attractions and state-of-the-art achievements in science and technology, all grouped around an artificial lagoon. Every 'village' consists of a number of buildings in the typical architectural style of the particular country, but only the sales personnel and hostesses in the pavilions, restaurants and souvenir shops are true representatives of their countries; the buildings seem a little too stereotypical. In the evening the lagoon is lit by the *IllumiNations* laser and firework show, set to classical music.

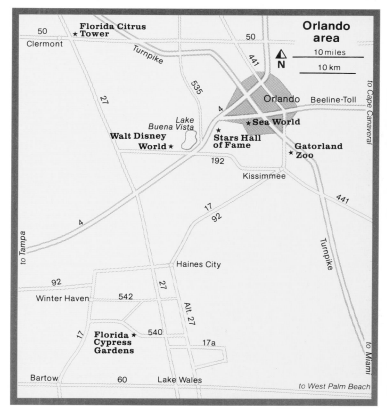

World Village sells luxury articles from almost all over the world.

 There are ten Walt Disney World resort hotels. The most spectacular is the futuristic *Contemporary Resort Hotel* (over 1,000 beds), where the monorail stops right in the lobby. There are the Tahitian-style *Polynesian Village Resort* and the *Disney Inn*, four more first-class hotels in the *Lake Buena Vista* holiday complex, and bungalows and treehouses in the *Lake Buena Vista Treehouse Village*. There are also the luxurious *Grand Floridian* and *Yacht Club* and the moderate *Caribbean Beach* and *Port Orleans* resorts.

Good sandy beaches have been created on the lakes near the Polynesian Village in *River Country* and on *Lake Buena Vista*.

You don't have to leave Disney World to go shopping, as there are many interesting shops near the amusements and in the *Disney Shopping Village*. Designer fashion by Pierre Cardin, quality glass- and ceramicware and elaborate jewellery are all available here. There are many curios for sale too: you can buy a carafe of 250-year-old Cognac, a stuffed giraffe or an antique fire-brigade pump.

First-class singers and dancers perform at the *Top of the World* in the *Contemporary Resort Hotel*. There are Country & Western shows in *Pioneer Hall, Fort Wilderness*, and a Tahitian-style show at the *Polynesian Resort*.

Fort Wilderness; all facilities.

Ocala Pop. 40,000
This town north of Orlando is well equipped for riding holidays. There are many stud farms in the area and the hilly countryside is ideal for riding. Many

World Showcase, Epcot Center

studs are open to the public and some offer complete riding-holiday packages.

Ex *Silver Springs* are deep blue lakes, supplied by subterranean spring water, set in a tropical jungle environment with many monkeys and birds. Trips in glass-bottomed boats, and jungle cruises on the *Silver River*. In the adjoining *Reptile Institute* there are daily displays with snakes and alligators. The *Early American Museum* reflects America's pioneering days. The exhibition of the early years of the automobile with numerous unusual vehicles is particularly interesting.

The Wild West comes to life in *Six Gun Territory*, a town between Ocala and Silver Springs, where there are mock gun-fights, bars and saloons with shows. *Ocala National Forest* is the only national park in the USA with subtropical vegetation. There are various campsites in the park, and well-stocked fishing grounds.

Epcot Center

The north-west

As yet not many tourists have ventured to the so-called 'Panhandle' of Florida where the state borders Georgia and Alabama on the Gulf coast from *Cedar Key* to *Pensacola*. However, the inhabitants of Florida and neighbouring states discovered the attractions of holidaying in the north-west long ago. And they were right: the beaches are quieter, the fishing grounds are richer here than anywhere else and the holiday centres of Panama City, Fort Walton Beach and Pensacola fulfil every requirement for an enjoyable holiday. This is also the location of Tallahassee, Florida's state capital. The 'Panhandle' is not the place to find the sun in winter; in December, January and February the average temperature is 56°F/13°C and a little chilly for sun-worshippers.

Tallahassee Pop. 88,000

Florida's state capital is situated inland almost exactly half-way between St Augustine and Pensacola. Tallahassee is not one of the most attractive towns in Florida but the modern administrative centre has strong links with the history of the southern states. The wealth and elegance of these states are reflected in the plantation-owners' residences on Park Avenue and Calhoun Street.

The Spanish erected a mission, *St Luis*, in 1633 on the site of the present city, to convert the Apalachee Indians to Christianity. In 1704 English troops destroyed the mission church and drove out the Indians. This event is recalled in the city's name, as Tallahassee means 'abandoned fields' in the

Great Seal of Florida in the Tallahassee State Building

Indian language. In 1824 Tallahassee became capital of the US territory of Florida and in 1845 the new state capital. During the American Civil War, Tallahassee was the only southern city east of the Mississippi to withstand the Union troops.

The main attraction is the *State Capitol*, Florida's seat of government, which combines an older building modelled on the Capitol in Washington and a modern administrative high-rise building between Monroe and Adams Streets. There is an excellent panoramic view from the 22nd floor of this skyscraper. The Capitol is open to the public daily from 9 am to 4 pm. In the government district there are also picturesque old buildings which predate the Civil War. The *Tallahassee Junior Museum* (Museum Drive) shows life in 19th c. Florida and has been specially designed for children. The *Museum of Florida History* (R. A. Gray Building, Bronough Street) highlights milestones in the state's history from the dinosaur to the Indians and the white settlers.

 Tallahassee Municipal Airport is linked to many major US cities.

Ex 15 miles south, to *Wakulla Springs*, the deepest spring in the world, situated in a forest of cypresses. The great variety of underwater wildlife can be viewed from glass-bottomed boats.

Panama City

Panama City Pop. 45,000

The town, with a busy commercial port in St Andrews Bay, is an aspiring centre of industry. *Miracle Mile* is on the *Panama City Beach* peninsula. The beach is one of the longest and finest in Florida. The hotels and numerous amusement parks are mostly situated to the west of the town on the snow-white beaches. Towards Pensacola to the east the coastline is rocky and only in a few places suitable for bathing.

 Gulf World Aquarium with shows; a reptile and bird park. *St Andrews Recreation Area* lies among high sand dunes on the beach and offers excellent facilities for hiking, swimming, diving and sailing. A renovated old hostelry is open to the public.

 Extensive beach of fine sand.

 Complete range of sporting activities in Panama City Beach.

Rodeos are held regularly in the Panama City area. *Mud races* for cars and tractors are also staged.

Panama City Municipal Airport with air services within Florida and to some major US cities.

Ex South-east of Panama City lies the small town of *Apalachicola*. Most of Florida's oysters come from here; visit a Raw Bar if you like this delicacy.

Fort Walton Beach Pop. 22,000

Until 1940 there were more black bears than people in Fort Walton Beach. Nowadays the town on Choctawhatchee Bay is a popular resort with some of the best fishing waters. North of Fort Walton is *Eglin Air Force Base*, one of the largest military complexes in the world. A visit to the base is very interesting, and there

Fort Walton Beach

are two-hour tours in summer (tour timetable available in the town). In the *Indian Temple Mound Museum* (Miracle Strip) there are ancient Indian burial mounds and artefacts made by the first inhabitants, who came here some 3,000 years ago for the rich fishing grounds. In the *Gulfarium* on Okaloosa Island there are displays with dolphins, seals and sea-lions. The museum of marine life, where a diver describes the various sea creatures, is also worth a visit.

This section of coast is also known as Miracle Strip thanks to its emerald-green water and fine sandy beach.

There is an annual 'fishing rodeo' (each October) in Destin, 5½ miles to the east.

Air services within Florida from *Fort Walton Beach Municipal Airport.*

Pensacola Pop. 68,000
Pensacola is Florida's extreme north-western town. From here it is a few minutes' drive to Alabama. The remnants of its rich history can be seen everywhere. Nowadays Pensacola is a modern resort with all amenities, but it has still retained its individuality.

The first Spanish settlement was founded as early as 1559 but was abandoned after two years. In 1752 a permanent settlement was established and named *Peñiscola* after the Spanish port. Up to 1864, control of the town passed through many hands, and in total five different nations flew their flags over Pensacola: Spain, England, France and the American Confederates and Unionists.

 What to see
Seville Square with its many pictur-esque 18th and 19th c. buildings is the most attractive part of Pensacola. The *Pensacola Escapades* sightseeing train tours the historic Old Town and the villas of *North Hill Preservation District*.

Also worth seeing are the *Naval Air Station*, with a museum of naval aviation history, and *Fort Pickens* on *Santa Rosa Island*, built in 1834. The famous Apache chief Geronimo was held captive here. The *US Naval Aviation Museum* is also worth visiting. Its exhibits include forty historic planes and a space capsule. There are daily bus tours from the museum to nearby historic combat sites. Not far from here is the *Sherman Field* air-force base, the home of the world-famous 'Blue Angels' aero-batics team, with displays throughout the year of their (rather noisy!) formation flying.

The exhibits of the *Pensacola Historical Museum* are housed in the *Old Christ Church*.

Gulf Islands National Seashore is the 150-mile strip of islands off Pensacola Bay stretching to Gulfport (Mississippi); many parts are nature conservation areas.

Hear Dixieland Jazz in *Rosie O'Grady's Goodtime Emporium*.

Pensacola's *International Airport Hagler Field* is used by many major US airlines.

Spanish Wells

Introducing the Bahamas

The 'heavenly beauty' of the Bahamas is to be found not only on its many small islands but also in the surrounding crystal-clear waters. The water ripples with silver in the bright sunlight, the colours extend like an exotic carpet of green, brown, beige and pink, with the white breakers followed by pale blue and turquoise out to the inky blue of the deep sea.

The many colours reflect the myriad features of the underwater world with its flat sandbanks, fields of sea grass, coral reefs and deep valleys. When island-hopping and flying low in the small planes, you can see not only yachts, cruisers and fishing boats below, but at times also big fish such as marlin, barracuda, tuna and dolphins.

White, beige and pink are the colours of the sand on the beach. The pink sand is not a trick of the light: it comes from the red coral, eroded with time and ground down by the waves and wind to a fine powder which is washed on to the shore.

The green is the extensive bushy jungle, full of humming-birds, orchids and an exotic vegetation of palms, bamboo, firs, pines, cypresses, mahogany and bread-fruit trees. Dotted around are cultivated areas of fruit and vegetables such as avocado, aubergine and pineapple.

In between lie lagoons and lakes, the playground of countless aquatic birds. Pelicans dive for their food while the large frigate birds circle high above.

The settlements, the wooden villas in typical English colonial style and the bright, constantly repainted houses and cabins of the black population are all as colourful as toy buildings. Even though the Bahamas have been more or less independent since 1964 and since 1973 have formed an independent republic, the English presence here for hundreds of years is still very much in evidence. This influence is expressed in the usually strict observation of Sunday as the 'day of rest', the discipline of drivers, the standard of dress expected in the better restaurants at night, the police uniforms and the judges' robes of office. There are also reminders of the era of Spanish and French pirates, and more recently the American way of life has left its mark. The mainly black population adds to the mix its more easy-going style of living.

If breakfast is advertised from 7.30 am you cannot expect it to be ready before 8. The taxi ordered for a specific time may be fifteen minutes late, half an hour late or may not even turn up at all, at least in Nassau. It is different on the more remote and less populated islands where everybody knows everybody else.

There are altogether great differences between the two main tourist islands, New Providence and Grand Bahama, and the outlying Family Islands, where the natural surroundings are basically unspoilt and the amenities for tourists mostly limited to watersports and a couple of tennis courts. There are, it is true, quiet areas on the south coast of New Providence, and at various points on Grand Bahama, particularly on the east coast.

None of the islands possesses grandiose cultural shrines or collections of major art treasures. There are a few caves bearing traces of the first inhabitants, the Arawak Indians, some reminders of Columbus and the pirates, the remains of landowners' residences and their slave quarters, a couple of old forts and light-houses and some more or less simple churches dating from the last century.

Holidaymakers have a choice between the 'designer' holiday centres of Freeport/ Lucaya and Nassau and surroundings, and the Family Islands; on the one hand the lively business of tourism with a wide range of accommodation, restaurants and sports complexes, well-maintained golf courses, busy marinas and the 'high life', and on the other a less expensive lifestyle closer to nature. People who seek peace and quiet and secluded beaches, who enjoy fishing, snorkelling or diving, will want to spend their holidays here.

Many people cruise among the islands on their own yachts or chartered yachts, and a number of large cruise liners call at the Bahamas, mainly at Nassau and Freeport. But visitors will only ever discover the real attraction of the Bahamas when sailing, deep-sea fishing or diving, activities which can turn a holiday into an expensive proposition. People who enjoy these holiday pursuits and can afford them will find no other place in the world to beat the Bahamas.

Essential details in brief

Name:

The Commonwealth of the Bahamas.

Area:

More than 700 islands and islets, with a total area of 5,358 sq miles; some 2,000 reefs and sandbanks also belong to the Bahamas.

Situation:

495 miles north of the Equator, between 21° and 27° latitude and 73° and 80° west longitude. The USA is only 50 miles away at the nearest point. The Bahamas extend over 745 miles from the east coast of Florida and the north coast of Cuba far into the Caribbean Sea.

Administration:

The former British Crown Colony, which gained independence on July 10th 1973, is a parliamentary democracy with a House of Assembly, Senate, autonomous jurisdiction and a Cabinet led by the Prime Minister. The Bahamas belong to the British Commonwealth of Nations and recognise Queen Elizabeth II as Head of State, represented by a Bahamian Governor General.

Population:

The population totals 240,000. 29 of the islands are inhabited; 136,000 people live on New Providence Island, 33,500 on Grand Bahama. 85% of the population are black, 15% white, of mainly British extraction.

Largest towns:

Nassau, pop. 140,000; Freeport, pop. 30,000.

Economy:

Tourism is the most important source of income. As a tax haven and financial focal point, the island state has developed into an important international centre for banking and insurance. The Bahamas also act as a drug distribution centre for the American market. Fish, crustaceans – especially lobster – and their processing also play an important role in the economy. Tropical fruits and vegetables are cultivated but exported only in limited quantities. Shipbuilding, salt, rum and mineral oil complete the limited range of industry on the Bahamas.

Signposts of history

Early history: The first inhabitants are Arawak Indians who come to the Bahamas in the first millennium AD.

October 12th 1492: During his search for the sea route to India, Columbus discovers the island of *San Salvador* or *Samana Cay*.

Early 16th c: The Spanish carry off the majority of the natives to work in the mines on Hispaniola (Haiti) or as pearl-divers on Trinidad. A Spanish expedition led by Ponce de León lands on several of the Bahamian islands and the area is called *bajamar* in Spanish, meaning shallow sea, and presumably the origin of the name Bahamas.

16th c: The sea route from Europe to the Caribbean passes through the shallows of the *Bahama Banks*. Among others, seventeen Spanish ships are stranded off *Abaco* in 1595.

From 1629: The English Kings Charles I and Charles II grant rights of ownership of the Bahamas to some of the nobility.

1645–50: Religious conflicts on the Bermuda islands force English Puritans to move to one of the Bahamian islands, which they call *Eleuthera* (meaning freedom in Greek).

1666–70: More English settlers arrive from Bermuda and America with their slaves.

Around 1670–1732: English, Dutch and French buccaneers use the Bahamas as their base. Ships are lured on to sandbanks by false beacons and plundered. Captain Woodes Rogers temporarily restores law and order as the first English Governor.

1776—84: During the American War of Independence some 10,000 loyalists to the English cause move to the Bahamas with their slaves.

1834: The Emancipation Act liberates all slaves.

1848: The *Turks and Caicos* Islands separate from the Bahamas.

1861/62: During the American Civil War the northern states blockade the ports of the southern states. Blockade-running ships loaded with weapons and food supplies operate out of Nassau, which brings prosperity to the islanders.

From about 1880: The beginnings of tourism on the Bahamas. In 1898 Henry Flagler in Miami creates a passenger-ship link between Florida and Nassau, and builds a hotel in Nassau.

1919–33: During Prohibition in the USA, *Grand Bahama* and the *Biminis* become the base for highly profitable alcohol smuggling.

1940: Edward VIII, as Duke of Windsor following his abdication, comes to the Bahamas as Governor.

1964: The Bahamas are granted extensive autonomy.

1967: Lynden O. Pindling becomes the first black Prime Minister.

July 10th 1973: The Bahamas gain independence and become a member of the United Nations, but remain in the British Commonwealth.

1989: Tourism reaches a new peak of 3.4 million visitors; the figure for 1965 had been 720,000 (mainly from North America). The numbers of European visitors are now growing from year to year.

✕ Food and drink

In an island state situated among the richest fishing waters of the world, seafood – fish, crayfish, crabs and other crustaceans – naturally plays a very important role. Dishes are often based on the meat of the large conch shellfish, more so in fact than in Florida, with which the Bahamian cuisine has much in common.

The *conch* forms part of the staple diet of the Bahamas, and since recent attempts to farm it have been successful, there are ample supplies even with the extra demand of tourists. It is prepared as *conch chowder* (a spiced soup with vegetables); *conch salad* (raw with onions, cucumber, tomatoes and celery in lemon-juice and seasoned with pepper); *cracked conch* (steamed then fried in batter, sometimes served with a hot lemon sauce); *conch fritters* (marinated and deep fried); *steam conch* (steamed then roasted with tomatoes, onions, celery, green peppers or other vegetables); *conch mayonnaise* (steamed, puréed and mixed with hard-boiled eggs, onions, pepper, mustard and mayonnaise); and also in countless other ways.

The most common fish, the *grouper*, is also prepared in every imaginable way.

Steaks, hamburgers and hot dogs, 'imports' from America, are often on the menu, particularly in hotel restaurants and beach bars.

Fruit, especially tropical fruit, forms the main dessert, whether served fresh, stewed, as fruit salad or in cakes, pies or tarts.

The rum-based cocktails are very similar to those served in Florida. The local beer *Kalik* is popular, as is the range of European lagers. Californian sweet and dry wines are reasonably priced; French and German wines are very expensive. There is American-style coffee and Bahamian coffee, which is strong and good.

Conch fisherman

Lobster Angostura, a local Bahamian recipe.

Boil 1 lb of spiny lobster in water. Melt 5 dessert spoons of butter in a frying pan; add 2 dessert spoons of finely chopped mild onion and simmer over a low heat until the onions begin to soften; stir in 4 dessert spoons of flour and gradually add 2½ cups of milk. Season with a little salt and pepper and add ½ a teaspoon of Angostura Bitters and half a cup of chopped almonds. Cut the meat into bite-size chunks and add to the sauce. Put the mixture into individual oven-proof ramekins and bake at 220°C in a pre-heated oven until golden brown.

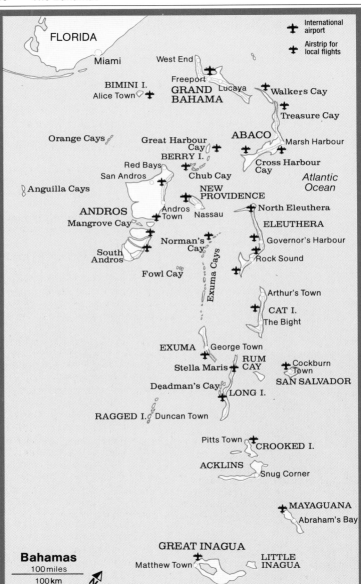

International airport

Airstrip for local flights

FLORIDA

Miami

West End

Freeport

Lucaya

BIMINI I.

Alice Town

GRAND BAHAMA

Walkers Cay

Treasure Cay

Orange Cays

Great Harbour Cay

ABACO

Marsh Harbour

BERRY I.

Red Bays

San Andros

Chub Cay

Cross Harbour Cay

Atlantic Ocean

Anguilla Cays

ANDROS

Andros Town

NEW PROVIDENCE

Nassau

North Eleuthera

Mangrove Cay

ELEUTHERA

Governor's Harbour

South Andros

Norman's Cay

Rock Sound

Fowl Cay

Exuma Cays

Arthur's Town

CAT I.

The Bight

EXUMA

George Town

Stella Maris

RUM CAY

Cockburn Town

Deadman's Cay

SAN SALVADOR

LONG I.

RAGGED I. Duncan Town

Pitts Town

CROOKED I.

ACKLINS

Snug Corner

MAYAGUANA

Abraham's Bay

GREAT INAGUA

LITTLE INAGUA

Matthew Town

Bahamas

100 miles

100 km

Where to go and what to see

New Providence — the capital island

New Providence occupying an area of 80 sq miles (21 miles long and up to 6½ miles wide) ranks as only the eleventh island in size of the Bahamas group, yet a good half of the total population of about 240,000 live here. Nassau, the capital of the island and the nation, is the seat of almost all the administrative and governing bodies of the Commonwealth of the Bahamas, and is also a major financial centre by virtue of its strict observation of banking secrecy.

Cruise liners from various countries put in at Nassau almost daily, some forming a regular link between the USA and the Bahamas.

Nassau International Airport is the largest (and only intercontinental) airport in the islands. Almost two-thirds of foreign visitors to the Bahamas spend their holidays on New Providence. Owing to its location near the centre of all the major tourist islands and its importance as the main air terminal, visitors almost always stop here on their way to the other islands. On New Providence visitors from the USA and Canada predominate, but the proportion of European tourists, particularly German, is greater here than on Grand Bahama and the Family Islands.

New Providence has a wide range of sports amenities, and is a particularly good centre for diving and fishing. Entertainment is also well catered for; the shows 'Le Cabaret' in the Paradise Island Resort and Casino and 'Les Fantastiques' in the Cable Beach Hotel and Casino bear comparison with what you would find in Las Vegas or Paris. The selection of holiday accommodation and restaurants ranges from simple town lodgings to bungalows and luxury hotels, and from little fish-bars to gourmet restaurants.

There are of course a large number of shops, boutiques and shopping centres in Nassau. Some things may be cheaper on, for example, the American Virgin Islands, and the Bahamas can hardly compete with international centres like Hong Kong or Singapore; nevertheless, some items such as perfume and jewellery are cheaper here than in Europe. The real assets on New Providence, though, are sports, recreation and entertainment.

The two most important holiday centres of the island are the offshore *Paradise Island*, connected by a road bridge, and the *Cable Beach* area, west of Nassau town centre, with modern hotels and a second casino. In the north-eastern part of the island there are mainly marinas but also some hotels. Paradise Island is Nassau's elegant annexe. Admission into this particular paradise costs two dollars on the toll bridge and four dollars by boat. The island offers good hotels and restaurants, a Club Méditerranée, well-maintained sports facilities, a casino and, in front of this, the impressive coral *Sea Gardens*. On the small island of *Silver Cay*, at Arawak Cay, is *Coral World Bahamas*, with large aquaria, an observation tower and small apartment-style hotel.

 New Providence was for a long time the favourite haven of Spanish, English and French pirates, thanks to its good natural harbour and hidden anchor-grounds. The Spanish occupied the island 'officially' in 1641 and on numerous later occasions. From 1666 English settlers from Carolina on America's east coast and from the Bermuda islands established themselves here.

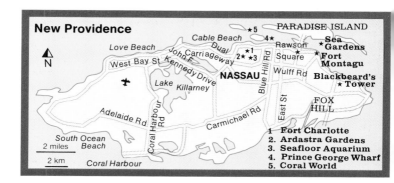

New Providence

PARADISE ISLAND

Cable Beach
Love Beach
West Bay St
John F. Kennedy Drive
Dual Carriageway
NASSAU
Lake Killarney
Adelaide Rd
Coral Harbour Rd
Carmichael Rd
Blue Hill Rd
Wulff Rd
East St
Rawson Square
★5
4★
★1
2★ ★3
Sea Gardens
★Fort Montagu
Blackbeard's ★ Tower
FOX HILL

South Ocean Beach
Coral Harbour

2 miles
2 km

1 **Fort Charlotte**
2 **Ardastra Gardens**
3 **Seafloor Aquarium**
4 **Prince George Wharf**
5 **Coral World**

They called the island *Sayle's Island* after the leader of the first immigrants to Eleuthera, and named the settlement *Charles Town* in honour of Charles II. The town was renamed Nassau in 1695 during the reign of William III of the House of Orange-Nassau. During the American War of Independence, Nassau was occupied for a few days by an American naval unit under the command of Commodore Ezekiel Hopkins. In 1783 the Bahamas were declared a British colony once again, a status which New Providence retained until independence was granted in 1973.

 What to see

There is a lot to see here and consequently a whole range of organised sightseeing tours and guided walks are provided. The government trains and supervises a number of tourist guides known as *Bahamahosts*. There are taxis (at fixed prices), horse-drawn carriages, scooters and bicycles available for people who wish to explore on their own.

Nassau. Most of the well-known sights are accessible on foot as they are situated in the town centre opposite the main harbour, *Prince George Wharf*, and

thus suitably convenient for cruise passengers. A tour of the most important sights takes about three hours.

Rawson and Parliament Squares. The two squares merge, forming the centre of the town and a focal point for tourists. The horse-drawn carriages are picturesque; the statue of Queen Victoria and the colonial-style government buildings are worth seeing. The *Houses of Parliament (House of Assembly, Senate)* and the *Supreme Court* belong to the Government Buildings complex. Behind stands the old prison building which has been converted into a library designed in historic style. The *Tourist Information Centre* is also on Parliament Square, and the guided walking tours of the town begin from here.

Queen's Staircase. Behind Parliament Square you can reach the Queen's Staircase via Shirley Street and Elizabeth Avenue. The narrow stairway of 66 steps, hewn out of the rock by slaves, was at one time a protected route to Fort Fincastle. Nowadays this small, romantic passage bustles with souvenir traders, artists and photographers. The artificial waterfall and floodlights are not always in operation.

Fort Fincastle and Water Tower. At the top of the staircase stand the fort, erected in 1793, with its small *Museum of Junkanoo* (the Bahamian carnival), and the *Water Tower*. The 126-ft-high tower is the highest point on the island and commands an excellent panoramic view (lift; open 9 am to 5 pm).

Government House. From the Water Tower continue along East Street and East Hill Street, with fine old colonial houses, to Government House, the residence of the Governor General. In front of the residence is a statue of Columbus looking out to sea. There is a ceremonial changing of the guard here at 10 am every second Saturday, accompanied by the band of the police force in historic uniform.

Government House, Nassau

Fort Fincastle – view to centre and harbour, Nassau

Strawmarket. From Government House, George Street leads directly to the Strawmarket, housed in the two-storey arcades of the Ministry of Tourism and extending along the harbour. From here it is worth going the short distance to the old British *Colonial Hotel* to have a drink in the garden.

Bay Street, the main shopping street where tax-free goods such as Scotch whisky and French perfume are on sale, leads back to Rawson Square.

Further west
If you have more time to spare, you can go westwards by taxi or on foot from the Colonial Hotel or Rawson Square to explore the following sights.

Nassau Botanic Garden. Tropical botanical garden with many varieties of flowers and plants, small ponds, cactus gardens and a children's playground.

Ardastra Gardens. The only trained flamingos in the world. It is amazing with what precision they respond to the commands of Joseph Lexion, their trainer. Apparently they take a dislike to bare female legs (perhaps jealousy?) so shorts and mini-skirts are taboo. Displays daily at 11 am and 4 pm.

Seafloor Aquarium. A large aquarium with sharks, giant turtles, trees of living coral, and other sea creatures. Displays by sea-lions and dolphins, Mondays to Saturdays 10.30 am, 12.30, 2.30 and 4.30 pm; Sundays 4 pm only. It is a short way from here to Fort Charlotte.

Fort Charlotte. The largest fort on the Bahamas, built in 1788, with a superb view of the port. Tour guides wear historic British/West Indian regimental uniform.

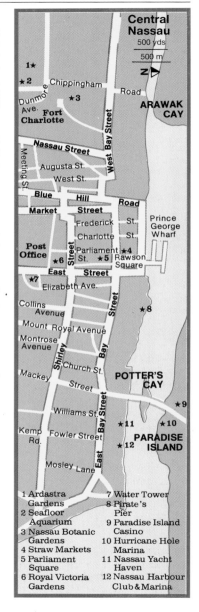

Central Nassau

1 Ardastra Gardens
2 Seafloor Aquarium
3 Nassau Botanic Gardens
4 Straw Markets
5 Parliament Square
6 Royal Victoria Gardens
7 Water Tower
8 Pirate's Pier
9 Paradise Island Casino
10 Hurricane Hole Marina
11 Nassau Yacht Haven
12 Nassau Harbour Club & Marina

Coral World is a fascinating underwater observatory with individual tanks of sharks, stingrays and turtles, and the largest artificially designed coral reef in the world, where marine flora and fauna live in a natural habitat. Visitors descend a spiral staircase to the observatory, which lies 20 ft below the water's surface and is one of the few places on Earth where you can walk into the sea without getting wet.

A particular attraction is the 98-ft-high steel observation tower with two terraces from which visitors may enjoy a clear view of Nassau, Cable Beach and Paradise Island.

Cable Beach is the promenade of hotels on some of the finest beaches on the island, which however are privately owned. On *West Bay Street* there are recording studios where the Beatles, the Rolling Stones and Eric Clapton have made records.

The north-east

There is also quite a lot to see in the north-east of New Providence, including the following.

Fort Montagu is the oldest of Nassau's three forts, and was built in 1741.

Blackbeard's Tower. The ruin of an old watchtower which, according to tradition, was erected by the infamous pirate captain Blackbeard (Edward Teach) as a look-out for new booty.

St Augustine's Monastery. Lying inland, the monastery and its school were designed by the legendary Fra Jerome in a neo-Romanesque style (see also Cat Island, page 84).

The south

The south coast has fewer attractions; there is a petrol refinery and a Bacardi rum distillery, offering visitors complimentary drinks.

Paradise Island Beach

Paradise Island

Just 3 miles long, Paradise Island faces Nassau harbour. The island has often been used as a film location, and is a sight in itself. Until the 1960s the island belonged to American multi-millionaire Huntington Hartford who erected a succession of luxury hotels here. Even if your finances will not stretch to a holiday on the island, try to spend at least half a day here, crossing the toll bridge by taxi or taking the boat from Nassau. It is also worth walking across Paradise Island Bridge for the wonderful view of the port and town. Under the bridge on Potter's Cay is the fish, fruit and vegetable market, which is supplied with wares by boat from the Family Islands. The elegant Paradise Beach is ideal for bathing. If walking seems too strenuous, you can explore the island by taxi or bus.

 What to see

Paradise Lake. A man-made lake fringed with palms, and connected to the sea by canals.

Casino. Gambling casino with theatre, nightclub, several restaurants and a shopping mall.

Versailles Gardens and French Cloister. Beautifully kept gardens in the French Baroque style with a number of monuments and statues, including a 13th c. statue of Hercules. In the centre of the gardens stand the impressive ruins of a French 14th c. Gothic Augustinian monastery. Huntington Hartford had the monastery dismantled in Montréjeau near Lourdes, transported to the Bahamas and reconstructed here.

Sea Gardens. Coral gardens off the south-east coast of Paradise Island, with many exotic fish and rich underwater flora. Tours in glass-bottomed boats (information available in hotels, and also in Nassau).

 Elegant beaches at *Paradise Island Beach* and at *Cable Beach*, the latter being the most frequented by tourists and situated some 3½ miles west of Nassau centre. Between the town centre and hotel district at Cable Beach are the *Western Esplanade* beaches (changing-cubicles, refreshments), and *Saunders Beach* and *Goodman's Bay*, visited mainly by local residents; *Montagu Beach* lies east of Nassau. *The Caves* and *Love Beach* in the west and *South Beach* to the south are more isolated.

 Several large marinas, also for fishing trips. *East Bay Street* in Nassau, *Hurricane Hole Marina* on Paradise Island.

Several fully equipped diving centres including instruction (addresses obtainable from the Tourist Information Centre). There are also good beginners' diving areas, at *North Rock Blow Hole, Rose Island Reefs* and

Mahoney Wrack. More experienced divers can use *Lyford Cay Drop-off* and *Clifton Pier Drop-off*.

 Boats at *Cable Beach* and on *Paradise Island*.

 Nassau Beach Hotel, Cable Beach Hotel and on *Paradise Island*.

 Cable Beach and *Paradise Island*.

 Carnival's Crystal Palace Golf Club and *Divi Bahamas*, both 18 holes.

 34 courts around Nassau, most at *Cable Beach*; 27 courts on *Paradise Island* and 20 at the *Club Méditerranée* (members only).

 Squash courts at *Nassau Squash and Racquet Club*, at the *Village Club* (sauna and pool) and at *Crystal Palace Hotel*.

Guided treks from *Happy Trails, Coral Harbour* and *Harbour Side Riding Stables*, Paradise Island.

Famous luxury restaurants include *Graycliff* (the landowner's residence dating from 1750 is regarded as one of the finest gourmet establishments; its visitors' book reads like a Who's Who of the jet-set); *Buena Vista* (historic rooms and garden terrace); *Da Vinci* (Italian and French cuisine); the *Regency* (Cable Beach Hotel). On Paradise Island: *Martinique, Courtyard Terrace* and *Villa d'Este* (Italian), *The Sun and...* (French and Bahamian cuisines).

Mid-range restaurants include: *Bridge Inn* (with music), *Captain Nemo's* (with music), *Poop Deck* (view of the harbour), *Tiffany's Restaurant* in the Gleneagles Hotel and *European Restaurant* in the Ocean Spray Hotel (both offer European cuisine).

Typical Bahamian restaurants: *Baha-*

mian Kitchen, Delaport Inn, Fish Net, Marietta's Restaurant, Le Shack (with music), *Traveller's Rest* (not far from the airport).

In Nassau and surroundings several discotheques and nightclubs, some with live music: *Fanta-Z, Sugar Mill Pub* in the Ambassador Beach Hotel, the *Patio Bar* in the Crystal Palace Resort & Casino British Colonial Hotel, Rendez-vous Lounge in the Britannia Tower on Paradise Island.

Bahama Rhythm Show Theatre, the *Junkanoo Lounge* in the Cable Beach Hotel, the *Drumbeat Club* near the Crystal Palace Resort & Casino British Colonial Hotel.

Revue in the *Le Cabaret Theatre* in the Paradise Island Casino (world famous) and in the *Cable Beach Casino.*

Large casinos on Paradise Island and at the Crystal Palace Resort & Casino (roulette, blackjack, baccarat and slot-machines; 1 pm–4 am; admission over 21).

The *Junkanoo* carnival on December 26th and New Year's Day (big procession on both days). Ceremonial opening of the Supreme Court Assizes with participants in historic dress: second Wednesday in January, first Wednesday in April and October. Miami–Nassau sailing regatta in February. *Labour Day Parade*: first week in July. International golf tournament in November.

Several air services daily from Nassau to Freeport/Grand Bahama, Miami, Orlando and other cities; daily services to Andros, Eleuthera, Abaco; several flights per week to the other Family Islands.

Tourist Information Offices on Parliament Square, at the Strawmarket, airport and Prince George Dock at the harbour. *Tourist News* information sheet.

Ex Apart from individual or organised excursions, there are boat trips to nearby islands and also excursion flights. Trips include a 'Robinson Crusoe tour' to a palm-tree island surrounded by reefs; visits to 'Treasure Island'; day cruises with refreshments and calypso music; trips on the *Calypso* to *Blue Lagoon Island* (many watersports amenities, music, buffet lunch); marine-life observation tours with the *Nautilus*, a small glass-bottomed boat (from Devaux Street dock); day trips to Grand Bahama and Miami; 2-day trips to *Disney World* in Florida; also *Air Taxi* private excursions (Nassau International Airport) to the Family Islands.

A special tip
Hartley's Underwater Wonderland organises yacht trips with underwater exploration of the sea-bed (with diving helmets; no previous experience necessary). You can feed the fish by hand and get a closer look at the coral flora.

Grand Bahama

In the 17th and 18th c. Grand Bahama was feared as much for its pirate stronghold as for its shallows. Only twenty years ago the islanders recovered several thousand gold and silver coins from the wreck of a Spanish galleon which sank in 1628 about half a mile off the coast during a storm.

Grand Bahama was a virtually uninhabited island of thick vegetation and forests until 1929 when the first lumberjacks arrived; even after that the settlements were sparse. During the years of Prohibition in the USA, particularly the mid-1920s, Grand Bahama gained importance for a time as a base for smugglers.

Grand Bahama began its career as a tourist centre in 1964 when the American timber-merchant Wallace Grove, who had established his business on the island, was able to realise the initial stages of his detailed and ambitious plans to develop an extensive holiday resort. Since then, Freeport/Lucaya has become the most important resort after Nassau, an American holiday colony offering 'sun, sand, sea and gambling'.

In this brief period of development, highly elegant, as well as more modest, hotels and bungalow complexes, extremely varied sports facilities, entertainment, gastronomic delights and shopping amenities have been created. Nowadays Grand Bahama boasts fourteen luxury hotels, five golf courses, fifty tennis courts, well-equipped diving and sports fishing centres, several marinas, two sophisticated casinos, the ingeniously designed International Bazaar, and gourmet restaurants offering international cuisine. The Port Lucaya shopping centre sells reasonably priced goods from all over the world. All these amenities are situated on a network of wide boulevards, set in magnificent gardens and enormous parks. Grand Bahama is particularly favoured by American tourists.

In 1940, 2,000 people lived on this island of about 540 sq miles; nowadays there are 30,000 inhabitants. The development of the island for tourism has been assisted by its proximity to the United States; it is only 55 miles from here to Florida. There are many daily charter flights as well as the airline services from Miami, Fort Lauderdale and Atlanta. Grand Bahama is keen to attract more European visitors, especially to the up-market Bahamas Princess Resort and Casino and the Lucayan Beach Resort and Casino.

 What to see

Various methods of transport are available for sightseeing: bicycles, mopeds, hire cars, taxis, tour buses and double-deckers. The main attractions are as follows.

Garden of the Groves. The botanical gardens dedicated to the founder of Freeport, Wallace Grove, and his wife contain trees, shrubs and flowers indigenous to the Caribbean, a small lake, three man-made waterfalls and a grotto (at Lucaya).

Grand Bahama Museum. Indian culture, old coins recovered from shipwrecks, and Junkanoo costumes.

Rand Memorial Nature Centre. Bahamian jungle as it was at the time of Columbus; rich birdlife. Guided tours Mondays to Thursdays and on Sundays (at Freeport).

Peterson Cay Park. Land and sea nature conservation area with coral gardens and rich marine flora and fauna. Scenic coral reefs may also be viewed from glass-bottomed boats.

El Casino. The casino in Freeport with its Oriental decor is also worth a visit, whether you wish to gamble or not.

International Bazaar. This shopping centre can supply virtually any item tax-free, but is worth visiting for its interesting architectural features alone.

 Several good beaches, near the hotel district in *Lucaya*, in *West End* and on the eastern tip of the island at *Deep Water Cay*.

 Large marinas, also for fishing trips, mainly at Freeport/Lucaya. Sailing yachts from the major hotels. Sunset cruises. Glass-bottomed boats from *Lucaya Beach*. The *Lucaya Water*way is ideal for a relaxing boat trip.

At the *Holiday Inn, Lucayan Beach Resort and Marina Hotel*, Lucaya.

At the *Atlantic Beach Hotel, Holiday Inn, Lucayan Beach Resort and Marina Hotel*.

At the *Atlantic Beach Hotel* (with instruction), *Lucayan Beach Resort and Marina Hotel*.

Very good diving areas through coral reefs and gardens. Fully equipped diving centres, including instruction, in Lucaya at *UnExSo*, in East End at the *Deep Water Cay Club*. Six trained dolphins accompany divers through the coral reefs, and tourists may swim and play with the dolphins for an additional fee.

In Freeport/Lucaya, five excellent 18-hole courses, all with restaurant or snack-bar, and instruction available.

21 courts in Freeport/Lucaya; the two *Princess Hotels* have six courts each.

Squash at the *Grand Bahama Tennis and Squash Club*.

Pinetree Stables, Freeport.

Speciality restaurants in Freeport/Lucaya are the *Bonanza* (Greek and American) and the *Café India* (Indian). The Princess Hotel offers a buffet on Wednesdays with dishes from around the world, and Polynesian cuisine in the *Mai Tai* at the hotel golf course. Well-known gourmet restaurants include the *Rib Room* and *Cotillon Room* in the Princess Hotels, the *Escoffier Room* in the Xanadu, the *Oasis* in the Princess Casino and the restaurant in the Lucayan Beach Resort. American and Bahamian cuisine in many hotels and other restaurants, including the *Stoned Crab*. Typical Bahamian restaurants in Freeport/Lucaya: *Basil's Seafood Restaurant, Village Gate, Fatman's Freddie's, Lobster House* and *Blackbeard's Rest* in the Garden of the Groves.

Taino Beach, Freeport

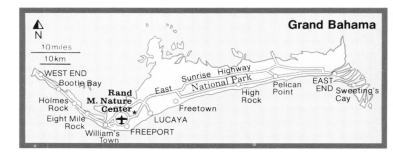

Grand Bahama

 Daily shows in the *Princess* and *Princess Tower*; on Wednesdays a *Goombay Festival* with traditional music and Bahamian buffet. Different programmes, including international shows, at *Castaways Resort*. Traditional music and dance in some hotels in Lucaya. The *Tide's Inn* at the Lucayan Bay Hotel offers a unique show combining underwater films and traditional music.

 Discotheques in many hotels; in some, live music and star guests.

Local handcrafted goods, particularly straw items, carvings and toys, in the Strawmarket.

 Large casinos in the *Princess Tower Hotel*, Freeport, and at the *Lucayan Beach Resort*. Slot-machines operate from 9 am. Roulette, blackjack and craps from noon to 3 am. Admission over 21.

Spectacular revues at the *Kasbah Theatre*, Freeport, and the *Flamingo Showcase Theatre*, Lucaya. Live entertainment at *Jack Tar Village*, West End.

Junkanoo on December 26th and New Year's Day. A sort of Caribbean carnival Bahamas-style, with plenty of music, bright costumes, dancing and a big procession.

 Information from hotels (also mopeds and scooters).

Several daily services to Nassau and Miami, several flights per week to Andros, Exuma, Long Island, San Salvador, Mayaguana, Inagua, Berry Islands, Crooked Island and South Caicos via Nassau.

i   Tourist Office, Freeport; International Bazaar.

Ex   Bus and boat tours from many hotels. Dinner cruises. Excursion flights to Nassau and most of the Family Islands.

A special tip

An exceptional shopping centre, the *International Bazaar* is a 10-acre complex by Hollywood architect Charles Perrin. There are Oriental, Indian, African, Mexican, Spanish, French and Scandinavian sections, each in the style of the respective country, with a number of restaurants and cafés. Goods from 25 countries are sold in the 70 shops. The jewellery centre at the exit displays copies of the English royal crowns since 1066, and of famous diamonds.

Treasure Cay

The Family Islands

The Abacos and Walker's Cay

The sickle-shaped main island of *Abaco*, hardly separated from its 'appendix' island *Little Abaco*, is surrounded by countless small islets and reefs. The scenery is very varied: flat and hilly, wide beaches and cliffs, bare open ground and dense vegetation in which live boars, wild ponies and many birds (parrot sanctuary in the south-east of the island).

Abaco, at 648 sq miles the second largest island of the Bahamas, is 130 miles long and up to 15 miles wide, but in places only a few hundred yards separate the east coast from the west. The average distance from Nassau is 75 miles, from Miami 200 miles. The population totals about 7,000. Some of the inhabitants are descendants of the English Loyalist settlers who came to the Bahamas with their slaves during the American War of Independence. Settlements such as *New Plymouth*, on *Green Turtle Cay*, and *Hope Town* are typical of the New England style.

Nearly all the settlements are situated on the east coast of Abaco or on the offshore Cays facing this coast. The tourist centres are *Treasure Cay*, the holiday peninsula, *Marsh Harbour*, the 'capital' of the island, *Hope Town* on *Elbow Cay*, *Great Guana*, *Green Turtle Cay* and *Walker's Cay*. This privately owned islet is a little holiday paradise in itself, with its own airport, which makes it quite exceptional. Accommodation on the Abacos ranges from simple fishing cabins to comfortable bungalows, villas and hotels.

 What to see

Hope Town. Not only a holiday resort

but also a local excursion favourite. It has a picturesque harbour and much-photographed red and white lighthouse; also the *Wyannie Malone Museum*.

A special tip
The ferry from Hope Town takes only a few minutes to reach Man-O-War-Cay, a picture-book village and the home of a religious sect who have earned a reputation as master boat-builders using traditional craftsmanship. They abstain from alcohol and tobacco, neither of which are available here.

New Plymouth on Green Turtle Cay. The bright, clean wooden houses with pointed roofs look as if they had just been painted; the town of the same name in Massachusetts may have looked like this 100 years ago. The *Albert Lowe Museum*, in a Victorian house, displays pictures and photographs on the history of the Abacos.

Cottman's House at Marsh Harbour. Dr Cottman, the author of *Out Island Doctor*, lived in this castle-like house which can be seen from far away (not open to the public).

Johnstone's Studio in Little Harbour. The home of a family of artists who have specialised in bronze work.

Wide beaches of fine sand at *Treasure Cay, Cherokee Sound, Hope Town* and on *Great Guana Cay*; smaller beach at *Great Abaco Beach Hotel*.

Boat hire of various classes (without crew). On the main island at *Treasure Cay Beach Hotel* and in *Marsh Harbour (Bahamas Yachting* with over 40 boats, *Windsong Marina*

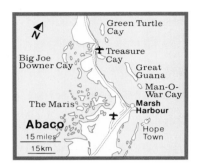

and *Boat Harbour Marina*); at *Great Guana Cay, Walker's Cay* and in Hope Town. Good reef and deep-sea fishing; boats with crews at *Guana Harbour Club*; island cruises from Treasure Cay.

The Abacos belong to the world's loveliest sailing areas. Yacht hire at *Pinder's Cottage*, Great Guana Cay and in Marsh Harbour, among other places.

 Terrific underwater world on view at the *Pelican Cays National Park* south-east of Marsh Harbour. Good diving areas: *Providence Channel, Devil's Hole* at Treasure Cay, *Spanish Cay*, and at *Man-O-War*, among others. Fully equipped diving centres at *Marsh Harbour, Green Turtle Cay, Hope Town, Treasure Cay* and on *Walker's Cay*.

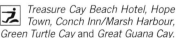 *Treasure Cay Beach Hotel, Elbow Cay Club, Green Turtle Yacht Club.*

Treasure Cay Beach Hotel, Hope Town, Conch Inn/Marsh Harbour, Green Turtle Cay and *Great Guana Cay*.

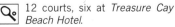 18-hole course in *Treasure Cay*.

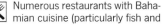 12 courts, six at *Treasure Cay Beach Hotel*.

 Numerous restaurants with Bahamian cuisine (particularly fish and crustaceans) including *Marsh Harbour Conch Inn, Mother Merle Fishnet* and *Great Abaco Beach Hotel.*

 Music daily at *Treasure Cay Hotel*, at the weekends at *Great Abaco Beach Hotel.*

 Fishing tournament in April, Abaco Festival Week in November.

 Marsh Harbour and Treasure Cay: daily services to Nassau and Miami.

Eleuthera, Harbour Island, Spanish Wells

The small islands of *Harbour Island, Spanish Wells* (both with several hotels) and *The Current* which lie just off the north coast of Eleuthera are generally grouped with it in tourist parlance.

Eleuthera

Eleuthera, 110 miles long and at no point wider than 2 miles, has three tourist centres, *Governor's Harbour, Rock Sound* and *Gregory Town*. Eleuthera is Nassau's most heavily populated 'neighbour' (it is 58 miles away) with 10,000 inhabitants. Chicken-farming, dairy products, and orange-, tomato- and pineapple-cultivation (near *Gregory Town*) are, together with tourism and fishing, the main sources of income.

 What to see

Preachers Cave, the first refuge of a group of English Puritans, also known as the Eleuthera Adventurers, who moved to the island in the mid-17th c. to escape religious oppression on the Bermuda islands.

The Cave at *Hatchet Bay* has stalactites and stalagmites.

Ocean Blue Hole. A large natural ocean pool at Rock Sound where visitors can feed the fish.

Glass Window. The narrowest point on the island, between Gregory Town and Upper Bogne.

Tarpum Bay and Cupid Cay. Picturesque old Bahamian-style settlements.

Spanish Wells

The inhabitants, quite a number of them white, are considered expert seafarers. Their white-roofed, pastel-coloured houses are popular with photographers. No vehicular traffic.

Harbour Island

Called 'Briland' by the inhabitants, it is considered by connoisseurs to be the most beautiful island in the Bahamas. The hilly island with dense vegetation boasts miles of wide beaches of fine pink sand, from the red coral washed ashore and ground down over the centuries by the wind and waves. *Dunmore Town* is one of the oldest and most picturesque townships on the Bahamas with its many old English-colonial-style houses. A Club Méditerranée has been established at Governor's Harbour, offering its guests all sports amenities.

 Apart from the magnificent beaches on Harbour Island, there are several wide sandy beaches on Eleuthera, as well as small bays and cliffs with pounding surf.

  Good shallow, reef and deep-sea fishing. Boat hire, also for deep-sea fishing, on Harbour

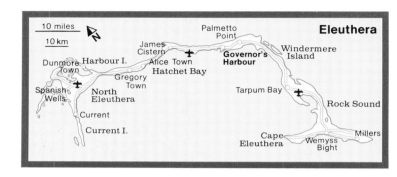

Island (*Valentine's Yacht Club, Romora Bay Club, Coral Sands Hotel*), on Spanish Wells (*Sawyer's Marina*), in Rock Sound (*Cotton Bay Club*) and at *Current*.

 Good diving areas with coral gardens, underwater caves and wrecks, including a 300-year-old ship with cannon in Yankee Channel and the oddity of a sunken locomotive, part of a cargo of railway coaches from a ship which went down years ago at *Devil's Backbone*. Fully equipped diving centres in *Rock Sound*, on Harbour Island and on Spanish Wells.

 Cotton Bay Club (Rock Sound) and Spanish Wells.

 On Harbour Island; and at Rock Sound, Governor's Harbour and Current.

 18-hole course in Rock Sound.

 On Harbour Island and in Rock Sound (11 courts).

International (usually American) and good local cuisine in most hotels and holiday complexes. Occasionally also Bahamian/Caribbean traditional music.

 Buccaneer Inn, Governor's Harbour.

Rock Sound, Governor's Harbour and North Eleuthera: daily services (sometimes several) to Nassau and Miami.

Exuma Islands and Cays

Some 140 miles separate the 71-sq-mile main islands of *Great* and *Little Exuma* from Nassau. The islands are surrounded by 365 Cays (most of them uninhabited), which effectively extends the Exuma archipelago northwards by almost 100 miles. The total population is about 4,000. The Exumas are among the best sailing areas in the world, and the 285-sq-mile *Exuma Cays Land and Sea National Park* comprises rich marine flora and fauna at depths of between 3 and 15 feet, and many birds and animals on land.

The small main town of *George Town* with its hotels *Out Island Inn, Peace and Plenty* and *Pieces of Eight* faces *Stocking Island*, which is uninhabited but during the day provides a bathing paradise with bars, barbecue areas, loungers, footpaths through the dunes and a glorious beach. Of the Exuma Cays, only *Staniel Cay* is of interest to tourists.

What to see

It is worth taking a trip to the north and south of George Town where you will encounter the name Rolle among inhabitants and village names alike. The biggest landowner on Exuma was Lord Rolle who set all his slaves free in 1835 and gave them land, on the condition that it should never be sold, but always passed on to the next generation. Many then adopted his name as a token of their appreciation.

Loyalist grave, Rolle Town

To the south

Go first to Rolle Town, situated on a hill with good views, which has three graves dating from the time of the English Loyalist settlers from the USA; continue to Little Exuma with its tiny settlements of *The Ferry, Forbes Hill* and *William's Town*. At William's Town are the ruins of an old mansion (*Cotton House*) and a large column which served as a landmark for cargo-ships collecting salt from the island.

To the north

Go via *Hermitage* (old graves among the trees) and the tiny village of *Gilbert Grant*, its early 19th c. colonial style virtually unaltered, to *Steventon* (more Loyalist graves) and *Rolleville*.

 Apart from the offshore bathing resort of *Stocking Island* at George Town (ferry from Out Island Inn

and Peace and Plenty hotel), many other secluded sandy beaches on Exuma and the Cays.

 Boats of various classes in George Town and Staniel Cay.

 Superb diving areas not only at the *Exuma Sea Park*, but also at *Thunderball Grotto* on Staniel Cay, *Mysterious Cave* at Stocking Island and the *Highborne Cay* area.

 Red Hill Plantation, The Ferry.

 Out Island Inn, George Town.

 *Kermie's Restaurant* near the airport at George Town (owner Kermit Rolle is also a taxi-driver and an ideal tour guide). *Peace and Plenty, Out*

Exuma

Plantation house, Little Exuma

Island Inn, Two Turtles Inn at George Town; *Happy People Marina*, Staniel Cay.

 Family Island Regatta in April: the regatta, from George Town round the Exumas, is a great local family event.

 Daily services from George Town to Nassau and Miami.

Andros

Andros, at 2,300 sq miles in area (up to 108 miles long and 45 miles wide), is the largest of the Bahamas and the nearest to Nassau (30 miles). Its population is 8,900.

Andros is a maze of waterways and lagoons which break the land into innumerable tiny islands and peninsulas, especially on the west coast. It is extensively covered with dense tropical vegetation and forest and is the most unspoilt island of the larger Bahamas. Almost all the settlements, supported by fishing and some vegetable cultivation, are situated on the east coast which is protected by a 117-mile-long barrier reef, the third largest in the world. Tourism is limited to smaller hotels and bungalow complexes (in total 500 beds); the main centres are *Congo Town, Mangrove Cay* and *Nicholl's Town*. Divers and anglers can find plenty to do off Andros's shores.

On no account should you laugh about the *chickcharnies*, the creatures of Indian legends which are said to inhabit Andros. These red-eyed apparitions with three fingers and three toes, and which are supposed to hang by their tails from the trees, cause mischief to anyone who does not treat them with respect.

 What to see

Numerous pretty little settlements, including *Nicholl's Town* (on the offshore islet of *Morgan's Bluff*, where the huge treasure of pirate Sir Henry Morgan is still said to be hidden in a cave), *Staniard Creek* and *Long Bay Cays* (with the grave of the infamous pirate Blackbeard). In *Red Bay Village*, the only settlement on the west coast, the inhabitants still live according to old tribal traditions. Inland, the island is rich in birdlife.

 Good extensive beaches, completely unspoilt, especially on the east coast.

Rich marine flora and fauna and lovely coral banks in the waters between the reef and east coast at depths of 12 to 18 feet, with the *Blue Holes* caves at up to 230 ft deep. Good diving areas also on the west coast south of *Yellow Cay*. Equipment hire, tank recharging, instruction and diving tours from *Small Hope Bay Lodge*, *Fresh Creek*, and the *Andros Beach Hotel*, Nicholl's Town.

Snapper, amber fish, perch, etc., inside the reef. Directly beyond the reef the depth plummets to 4,920 feet into the *Tongue of the Ocean* rift which is ideal for big fish such as blue marlin. The small *Lowe Sound Settlement* is one of the best areas in the world for big fish. Boats for deep-sea fishing at *Andros Beach Hotel; Chickcharnie Hotel*, Fresh Creek; *Small Hope Bay Lodge* and *San Andros Inn*. Smaller boats also at *Las Palmas*, Congo Town.

 San Andros Inn.

  In *Nicholl's Town* and *Congo Town*.

Two courts each (with floodlights) at the *Andros Beach Hotel* and *San Andros Inn* and Tennis Club; also at the *Las Palmas Hotel*.

In Nicholl's Town *Donna Lee, Andros Beach Dining Room, Paula's Inn, Henrietta Rolle, Hunder's* and *Eva Henfield*; in Mastic Point *Desert Inn* (spare ribs a speciality).

 Typical Bahamian *Goombay* music and Caribbean music in Nicholl's Town, including the *Andros Beach Hotel* and *Paula's Inn*; in San Andros in the *San Andros Hotel*. Traditional dancing at festivals, and sometimes just extempore on the beach.

 Fishing-boat regatta at *Mangrove Cay* in August.

 Frank Hanna's Shopping Centre, Nicholl's Town.

At the Andros Beach Hotel, Nicholl's Town.

Four airports; daily services from *San Andros* and *Andros Town*; from *South Andros* (near Congo Town) and *Mangrove Cay* several flights per week to Nassau, Small Hope Lodge/ Fresh Creek and Miami/Florida.

The Bimini and Berry Islands

The *Biminis* with about 1,500 inhabitants consist of North, South and East Bimini Islands and numerous uninhabited islets. In total they cover only 8½ sq miles. They are the nearest islands to Florida's coast, at 50 miles east of Miami. Near North Bimini there are lines of chiselled stones some 30 feet underwater, which some think belonged to the lost continent of Atlantis.

The *Berry Islands* covering 12 sq miles, and situated 150 miles from Miami and only 34 miles from Nassau, are an archipelago of 30 islands with only 500 inhabitants. Tourism here is concentrated on *Great Harbour Cay* and *Chub Cay*, and on the Bimini Islands at *Alice Town* on *North Bimini*.

The Bimini Islands

The strawmarket in *Alice Town* and *Blue Marlin Cottage*, where Hemingway lived from 1931–37, are worth seeing; the *Compleat Angler Hotel* has a Heming-

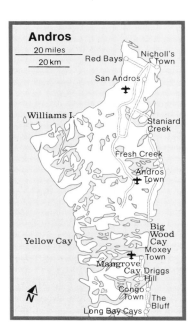

Andros

20 miles
20 km

Red Bays
Nicholl's Town
San Andros
Williams I.
Staniard Creek
Fresh Creek
Andros Town
Big Wood Cay
Yellow Cay
Moxey Town
Mangrove Cay
Driggs Hill
Congo Town
The Bluff
Long Bay Cays

N

way exhibition of manuscripts and pictures. In the *Lerner Marine Laboratory*, belonging to the US Museum of Natural History, many varieties of fish may be observed with underwater video cameras and special microphones. Near the air strip on South Bimini is the legendary *Fountain of Youth*, for which the Spanish seafarer Ponce de León searched without success in 1513.

 Good sandy beaches at Alice Town: *Paradise, Glory* and *Radio Beach*.

 The Biminis have some of the best fishing waters for marlin, tuna, and other big fish. Several fishing tournaments from March to August. Boats for deep-sea fishing at *Blue Water Marina* and the *Compleat Angler Hotel* (North Bimini) and at the *Bimini Island Yacht Club*, South Bimini. Smaller boats available from hotels. Harpoon fishing for large perch etc. near the numerous sunken shipwrecks.

 Several researchers consider that the unusual underwater stone formations could indicate the lost city of Atlantis. Diving gear at *Bimini Undersea Adventures*.

 At the *Big Game Fishing Club* and the *Bimini Inn*, both at Alice Town.

 At the *Big Game Fishing Club*.

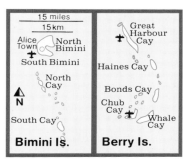 Several daily flights from Fort Lauderdale and Miami to Bimini by sea-plane; air link between Paradise Island and Bimini.

The Berry Islands
Chub Cay primarily attracts deep-sea anglers and divers, whereas *Great Harbour Cay* with its elegant hotels is a popular resort with visitors who seek greater comfort.

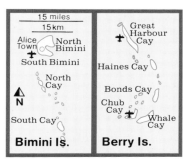

 Unspoilt beaches with vegetation and palm trees on many parts of the islands.

 Blue marlin are very common in the waters around *Chub Cay*. Boats at *Chub Cay Marina*. Blue marlin tournaments in July.

 Scenic *sea gardens* in the shallows south-east of Chub Cay. To the north, flat sandbanks with perch and snapper to be seen.

 Chub Cay Club.

 Bullock Harbour.

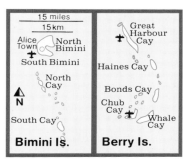 Two flights per week from Chub Cay to Nassau and Miami.

Cat Island

Cat Island is situated almost exactly in the middle of the island chain of the Bahamas, some 125 miles from Nassau. The island is 47 miles long and in many places only 2 or 3 miles wide. With its 50 miles of beautiful secluded sandy beaches, its cliffs, wooded hills and houses thatched with straw, it is one of the loveliest islands of the Bahamas. It also boasts the Bahamas' highest 'mountain' at 206 feet, *Mount Alvernia*, on which Fra Jerome built his hermitage. Though Cat Island has remained untouched by 20th c. civilisation to a large extent, there are some small-scale but good tourist amenities in the south.

There are several caves bearing traces of the first inhabitants, the Arawak Indians. In *Port Howe* stands the house of Colonel Andrew Devaux who retook Nassau from the Spanish in 1783. Hardly any visitor to Cat Island leaves without seeing the chapel designed by Fra Jerome in 1940.

   Boats, also for deep-sea fishing, and diving gear at *Hawks Nest Club* which has excellent scuba equipment, and at *Cutlass Bay* Club Hotel. Boats also from the *Greenwood Inn*, Port Howe.

  Fernandez Bay Village and *Cutlass Bay.*

 At the *Hawks Nest Club.*

 The hotels and clubs mentioned above all serve Bahamian and American cuisine, sometimes with traditional music. Good local cuisine also at the restaurants in *The Bight, Bennett's Harbour* and *Arthur's Town* in the north.

 Car rental through the hotels. Bicycle hire at Hawks Nest and Cutlass Bay.

 Flights from private air companies. *Bahamasair* services twice a week from Nassau to Arthur's Town.

Long Island

One of the better-known (and the most southerly) of the Family Islands, Long Island is 65 miles long and on average only one and a half miles wide, and lies some 155 miles from Nassau. More land is cultivated here than on the other islands, primarily for tomatoes, onions and pineapples. There are also more horses, cows, sheep, goats and pigs to be seen here, as well as old salt-pans which are still in use in the south. The 4,000-odd inhabitants have earned a reputation as boatbuilders. The main town of Long Island is *Clarence Town*; the tourist centre at *Stella Maris* lies further north.

 What to see

The two largest churches of the Family Islands, one Catholic, the other Anglican, stand in Clarence Town. Both neo-Gothic-style churches are the work of one man, Fra Jerome, an almost legendary figure, whose hermitage on Cat Island has become a tourist attraction. Fra Jerome, originally an Anglican, converted to the Catholic faith.

Of the many caves on Long Island, the most interesting is *Deadman's Cay Cave*, with stalactites and stalagmites and two ancient Indian wall-paintings.

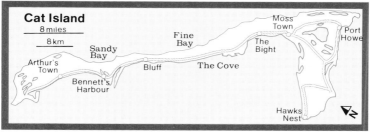

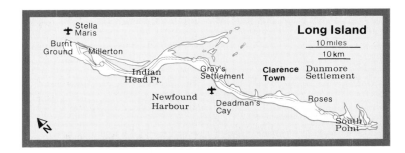

 Wide flat sandy beaches, but also a number of cliffs.

  Well-equipped diving centre in Stella Maris; compressors, tank recharging, equipment hire, several diving-boats (also with cabins for extended diving tours), and instruction.

   Stella Maris Inn.

 In the *Stella Maris Inn*; also Bahamian cuisine in *Conchy's* and in the *Marina Bar*; in the *Deadman's Cay* area, *Traveler's Restaurant*, *Kentucky No. 2* and *Thompson Bay Restaurant*.

Sailing regatta in June.

Long Island

Strawcraft in Stella Maris.

Several flights weekly from Stella Maris and Deadman's Cay to Nassau and Miami.

San Salvador and Rum Cay

These two small islands, *Rum Cay* at 18½ sq miles and *San Salvador* at 38 sq miles, lying 198 miles from Nassau, really deserve the over-used label of 'paradise'. Sandy beaches surround the gently undulating land, which is covered in flowering shrubs and different varieties of palm trees. A third of San Salvador is taken up by its 28 lakes, the largest of which is 12 miles long. On Rum Cay the population, less than 100, live by fishing and agriculture. Horses and carriages are used instead of cars. On San Salvador (population about 800) there are some signs of tourist development in the main settlement *Cockburn Town*, but still not many more than 100 hotel beds.

San Salvador

On October 12th 1492 Columbus is supposed to have landed south of Cockburn Town (a large cross marks the spot) and thus first set foot in the New World. (It is possible that his first landfall was in fact neighbouring Samana Cay.) Close to the cross is a monument commemo-

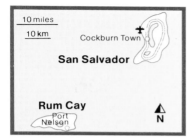

rating the 1968 Olympic Games in Mexico, when the Olympic flame was brought to San Salvador. The *Dixon Hill* lighthouse is also a popular sight.

 Riding Rock Inn near Cockburn Town is a centre for many sports. Excellent fishing grounds at *Pigeon Creek* where lobsters weighing up to 16lbs have been caught.

✈ Two flights per week to Nassau.

Rum Cay
It is probable that you will only travel to Rum Cay in order to visit the nature conservation area on neighbouring *Conception Island* – as did Queen Elizabeth II. There is evidence that Columbus also landed here.

Many aquatic birds live on Conception Island, many migrating birds stop here on their way from North to South America, and green turtles bury their eggs in the sand. The island can only be reached by boat from Rum Cay. You can get there by taking the very uncomfortable mail boat from Nassau via Cat Island.

The Southern Bahamas
At the southern end of the Bahamas lie the islands of *Crooked Island, Acklins*

Island, Mayaguana and *Great Inagua*, together with a great number of smaller islands and cays, of which twenty form the *Ragged Island* group (in total 8½ sq miles and 200 inhabitants). None of these islands have been developed to any great extent for tourism, and they thus retain their unspoilt quality.

Crooked Island and Acklins
Crooked Island, Acklins and *Fortune Island* (also called *Long Cay*), which lies off the south-west coast of Crooked Island, form a U-shaped group, its open end protected by a barrier reef. The enclosed shallow waters are known as the *Bight of Acklins*. Crooked Island and Acklins rise to a height of 165 feet and are covered with shrubs and plants whose characteristic scent was mentioned in Columbus' notes. Crooked Island, 69 sq miles in area and 230 miles from Nassau, is linked by ferry to Acklins (119 sq miles in area, 265 miles from Nassau). Both islands have air strips. Crooked Island and Acklins have made some progress towards tourist development.

 What to see
Bird Rock Lighthouse. It is worth driving out to the lighthouse on the northern tip of Crooked Island to watch the ships, as the *Crooked Island Passage* is one of the most frequented sea routes between the Atlantic and the Caribbean. *Colonel Hill* affords the best view over the island.
Caves of Crooked Island. The local inhabitants can show the way to a number of caves with unusual rock formations which, with a little imagination, look like ruined castles or churches.
Snug Corner and *Pompey Bay*. Two picturesque little settlements on Acklins.

Good sandy beaches on Crooked Island at *Landrail Point* and *Cabbage Hill*, and at *Pinefield* on Acklins. Also many isolated beaches on both islands.

 Boats, also for deep-sea fishing, at *Tands Guest House*, Cabbage Hill, Crooked Island and at *William's Hilltop View*, Pinefield, Acklins. Smaller boats at the *Pittstown Point Landings Inn*, Crooked Island.

 Fascinating diving and snorkelling areas at *Pittstown Point Landings Inn* on Crooked Island, where compressors, tank recharging, diving-boats and boat tours are also available.

 On Crooked Island, in Landrail Point *Gibson's Restaurant* and *Pittstown Point Landings Inn* (with Bahamian music), and in Colonel Hill *Happy Little Tavern* and *Hilltop Restaurant*.

 Several flights per week from Crooked Island and Acklins to Nassau via Exuma.

Great Inagua and Mayaguana
Great Inagua, the third largest island of the Bahamas covering 595 sq miles, and situated 360 miles from Nassau, is inhabited by 3,000 people and 14,000 flamingos. Economically, Great Inagua is important for its salt production. Legend has it that the tyrant King of Haiti Henri Christophe hid a horde of gold at the northern end of Great Inagua in 1820 before he shot himself. Little Inagua is uninhabited.

The few nature-lovers who venture to Great Inagua find accommodation, restaurants and some entertainment in the small settlement of *Matthew Town*.

Yachts sometimes anchor off neighbouring *Mayaguana* (110 sq miles, with some 600 inhabitants) for the sake of its beautiful beaches.

A special tip
Flamingos, which at one time were found all over the Bahamas, now have their last Bahamian preserve at *Lake Windsor* on Great Inagua, an extensive inland sea which is thought to be the world's largest breeding ground of these birds. The conservation area, covering 287 sq miles, is also the habitat of countless other birds and turtles. The *Bahamas National Trust* organises tours to see the flamingos and turtles.

One flight per week from Inagua via Mayaguana to Nassau.

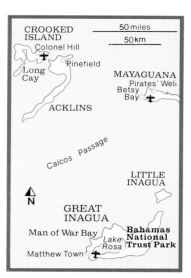

Useful things to know

For all visitors

Climate

The climate in the south, the most popular area, of Florida and in the Bahamas is similar, varying from around 86°F between June and September to around 75°F between December and February (Miami and Nassau). In the south of Florida, the temperatures on the Keys are about 1–1.5 degrees higher than on the west coast about 0.5–1 degree lower than on the east coast at Miami. There are similar variations in the Bahamas between southern and northern islands in relation to Nassau. The winter temperatures in the north and north-west of Florida are 6–8 degrees lower than those in Miami.

Rainfall in the south of Florida and the Bahamas is minimal between November and May. Rainfall during the other months is usually of short duration but heavy.

As far as the weather is concerned, the holiday season is year-round in the south of Florida and in the Bahamas. There is however a high season from December to April when tourists from North America and Canada migrate in numbers. If you are travelling in winter you should pack some warm clothing, and at other times it is advisable to take lightweight cotton garments, something warmer for the evening, and rain-gear.

For overseas visitors

Florida

Time

Florida has two time zones, *Eastern Standard Time*, which is GMT minus 5 hours, or during Daylight Saving Time (April 1st to the last Sunday in October) GMT minus 4 hours; and in the north-western corner *Central Standard Time*, which is GMT minus 6 hours, or during Daylight Saving Time GMT minus 5 hours.

Immigration and customs regulations

The US Immigration Service requires British visitors to be in possession of a valid UK passport; visitors from elsewhere may require a visa as well as a passport, and should check with their US Embassy. Every passenger is required to complete a customs declaration before entry into the US. Plants, meat products, soft cheeses and fruits may not be taken into the US. You may bring in 200 cigarettes, 50 cigars or three pounds of tobacco, gifts to a total value of $100, and one US litre of spirits.

Currency

Any currency up to a value of $1,000 may be taken into the US but visitors are advised to take only US dollars and travellers' cheques. Eurocheques are not accepted. It is hard to get by in the US without a credit card; the major cards are Visa, Eurocard and American Express. Cards with pin codes may be used in cash dispensers.

Dollar notes have one drawback: they are all the same size and colour and are easily confused. The dollar notes are in denominations of 1, 5, 10, 20, 50, 100 and 200. The coins are more easily distinguished, and their common names are: penny = 1 cent;

nickel = 5 cents; dime = 10 cents; quarter = 25 cents; half dollar = 50 cents.

There is also a one-dollar coin, though it is seldom used.

Getting to Florida by air

There are great price differences between the individual airlines, some offering whole package deals including car hire and accommodation. It is advisable to ask your travel agent about surcharges such as airport tax.

Driving in Florida

Florida has an excellent road network and caters well for drivers. Many sights are difficult to reach by public transport, if at all. It is cheaper to book cars or tourers before departure. All hire cars have automatic gear change.

Vehicles travel on the right; the maximum speed limits are 65 or 55 mph (as marked) on Interstates and Toll Highways, 55 mph on US and State Highways, and 25–30 mph in built-up areas. A valid UK driving licence is sufficient documentation for Britons driving in the US. It is advisable to have plenty of change for the toll roads.

Public transport

All major cities may be reached by *Greyhound Bus*. When using city buses, it is advisable to tender the exact fare as bus-drivers do not give change. In Miami you can travel by either *Metromover*, the rapid transit system in Downtown Miami which connects with the *Metrorail* to go to Hialeah and Coconut Grove, or by *Metrobus* (blue-green signs at the bus-stops). The railway network is not comprehensive.

Taxis

Taxis, or 'cabs', are not cheap. The charges must be listed in the vehicle and you should check that the meter is working.

Health insurance

Health care in Florida is excellent. There is no public health-care scheme in the US and treatment and medication must be paid for on the spot. It is advisable to take out medical insurance before departure (usually available as part of your holiday package). Emergencies are dealt with at the local hospitals' *Emergency Service*.

Post and telephone

Stamps are obtainable from the post office or (with a surcharge) from machines in shops and hotels. Telegrams may be sent from Western Union offices.

Telephone calls from coin-operated phones are cheaper; long-distance calls are connected by the operator. In emergencies, dial 0 for the operator or 911. Many organisations use freephone numbers.

Area codes:
305 Miami, south Florida and the Keys
813 Gulf coast and west Florida
407 Central Florida (Orlando)
904 North and north-west Florida
First dial 1, then the area code and the seven-digit subscriber number.

To telephone to the UK, dial 011 44, and omit initial 0 from area code.

Opening times

Opening times vary in shops; larger shopping centres are open 24 hours, smaller shops usually until 9 or 10 pm (also at the weekend). Banking hours are usually Monday to Friday 9 am to 5 pm, though some banks operate longer hours.

The information offices of the local Chambers of Commerce are open from between 8 and 10 am and close from between 6 and 9 pm.

Public holidays

New Year's Day (January 1st); *Washington's Birthday* (third Monday in February); *Memorial Day* (last Monday in May); *Independence Day* (July 4th, the principal national holiday, with fireworks and overcrowding in all holiday resorts!); *Labor Day* (first Monday in September); *Columbus Day* (second Monday in October); *Thanksgiving* (fourth Thursday in November); *Christmas Day* (December 25th). Good Friday, Easter Monday, Whit Monday and Boxing Day are *not* public holidays in the USA.

Hotels

Hotel rooms are not calculated per person but per double room. The prices vary considerably according to hotel category, location and season. Motels are somewhat cheaper and often have restaurants. Prices are usually only for accommodation; breakfast is charged separately.

Tipping

In the USA, service personnel, whether taxi-drivers, porters, waiters or chambermaids, make their wages almost exclusively from tips. In restaurants, a tip of 10–15% of the total bill is usual, after the unavoidable *State Tax*. Taxi-drivers expect 50 cents per trip.

Camping

There are over 800 campsites in Florida, most of which have all facilities.

Electricity

The voltage is 110 volts, 60 Hertz a/c; an adaptor is required for British electrical equipment.

Important addresses
Diplomatic offices

British Embassy
3100 Massachusetts Ave NW
Washington DC 20008
tel. 202 462 1340

British Consulate
Brickell Bay Office Tower
100 S. Bayshore Drive, Suite 1700
Miami FL 33131; tel. 305 374 1522

Canadian Embassy
1746 Massachusetts Ave NW
Washington DC 20036
tel. 202 785 1400

Australian Embassy
1601 Massachusetts Ave NW
Washington DC 20036
tel. 202 797 3000

New Zealand Embassy
37 Observatory Cir. NW
Washington DC 20008
tel. 202 328 4800

Irish Embassy
2234 Massachusetts Ave NW
Washington DC 20008
tel. 202 462 3939

Tourist information
In US

United States Travel and Tourism Administration (USTTA)
Department of Commerce
14th Street NW
Washington DC 20230
tel. 202 377 0136

Greater Miami Convention & Visitors Bureau
1601 Biscayne Boulevard
Miami FL 33132
tel. 305 350 7700

Florida Department of Commerce
Division of Tourism
Collins Building, Suite 530
Tallahassee FL 32399
tel. 904 488 3305

In UK

USTTA
Travel Information Centre
22 Sackville Street
London W1X 2EA; tel. 071 439 7433

The Bahamas
Time
GMT minus 5 hours.

Immigration and customs
UK citizens are not required to be in possession of a valid passport to enter the Bahamas for a period of up to three weeks but will need one to re-enter the UK. US visitors need an ID photo and proof of citizenship; a passport, though not required, can however be useful. A return or transfer ticket is required. No inoculations necessary.

50 cigars, 200 cigarettes or one pound of tobacco, one litre of spirits and one litre of wine may be imported duty free. The possession of illegal drugs is heavily penalised.

There are no currency restrictions, other than that the Bahamian currency may not be brought into the country. It is advisable to take US dollar travellers' cheques and US currency, which is accepted everywhere; Eurocheques are not accepted.

Currency and credit cards
The Bahamian currency is the Bahamian dollar (consisting of 100 cents) which has the same value as the US dollar. Credit cards are not as common in the Bahamas as in Florida, and they are often not accepted in the Family Islands.

Getting to the Bahamas by air
British Airways has a direct service from London. Travel agents will supply information about charter services, which often vary according to the season. There are many daily connecting flights from Miami with Bahamasair and other airlines. An airport tax of 7 US or Bahamian dollars per person, except children under 3 years of age, is levied on departure.

Transport within the Bahamas
There are good air links between the various islands, particularly from Nassau and Grand Bahama, mainly with *Bahamasair*. Flights take between 15 and 60

Walt Disney World

minutes. Some of the Family Islands also have scheduled flights with other airports. Special flights are arranged through a number of small charter companies operating from the international airports at Nassau, Freeport and Miami.

Mail boats also commute between the islands, but they are usually crowded, slow, uncomfortable and not recommended for the average tourist.

Cars may be hired on most of the islands; an international driver's licence is necessary. Vehicles travel on the left. Taxis are readily available but those on the Family Islands have no meters and charge fixed rates for standard trips.

Health care and medical insurance

If you require specific medication, you must take it with you. Particularly on the Family Islands, not all medication is available, or else it will take time to get there. Medical insurance is strongly recommended as medical services are costly on the Bahamas. Comprehensive travel insurance is of course advisable.

Hotels

The range of accommodation on the Bahamas is very broad. On the Family Islands the standard of accommodation does not at times rise above mid-range, but you find a more personal atmosphere and lower prices. The Bahamas are not cheap. If you have pre-paid accommodation or are in possession of a booking confirmation, you are protected by the new regulations of the hotel association. Whenever a guest cannot be accommodated in one hotel for any reason, the guest must be provided with alternative accommodation and any surplus charges met on his behalf. On New Providence and Paradise Island there are a number of hotels with special facilities for the disabled.

Note that the title 'Club' often refers to nothing more than a simple bar, particularly on the Family Islands.

People-to-People programme

This programme enables visitors to meet local families with similar interests and is organised by the *Ministry of Tourism*, PO Box N–3701, Nassau, or through the Tourist Information Centre in Nassau or Freeport/Grand Bahama.

Opening times

Banking hours in Nassau and Freeport are Monday to Thursday 9.30 am to 3 pm, Friday to 5 pm. On the Family Islands the hours vary; often the banks are only open in the mornings, until 1 pm.

The shops on New Providence and Grand Bahama are usually open Monday to Saturday 9 am to 5 pm. On the Family Islands there are no set opening times.

Post and telephone

Airmail to and from the Family Islands is often transported to and from Nassau with the mail boat and can take weeks to arrive.

Telephone connections are relatively quick day and night from New Providence, Grand Bahama and some of the Family Islands, but extremely difficult from some of the smaller islands.

Weights and measures

UK Imperial system.

Electricity

Generally 120 volts; US appliances are compatible, but British ones require an adaptor.

Souvenirs

Typical souvenirs include handcrafted straw goods and wood-carvings, Androsia batik fabrics, and mother-of-pearl jewellery.

Public holidays

New Year, Christmas Day, Boxing Day and Independence Day (July 10th) are fixed dates; Good Friday, Easter Monday and Whit Monday are moveable feasts. Also *Labour Day* (first Friday in June), *Emancipation Day* (first Monday in August) and *Discovery Day* (second Monday in October).

Junkanoo

The most boisterous of the Bahamian carnivals, Junkanoo, is celebrated everywhere in the Bahamas, particularly in Nassau and Freeport/Lucaya, on December 26th and New Year's Day. The locals dance through the streets (they call it 'rushing') in bright costumes, mostly made of paper. Prizes are awarded for the best costumes. Musical accompaniment is provided by goat-skin drums, pipes, horns and cowbells.

Important addresses

Diplomatic offices

UK High Commission
PO Box N–7516
Bitco Bldg., E. Street
Nassau; tel. 325 7471

US Embassy
PO Box N–8197
Queen Street
Nassau; tel. 322 4733

Tourist information

Ministry of Tourism
PO Box N–3701
Bay Street
Nassau; tel. 322 7500

Bahamas Tourist Offices

In UK
10 Chesterfield Street
London W1X 8AH; tel. 071 629 5238

In US
150 E. 52nd Street
New York, NY 10022
tel. 212 758 2777

Index

Abacos   77ff.
Acklins   87f.
Alice Town   83
Ana Maria Island   44
Andros   82f.

Bahia Honda   16
Berry Islands   83f.
Big Pine   16
Biminis   64, **83f.**
Boardwalk and
    Baseball   53
Bradenton   43f.
Bradenton Beach   44
Brighton Seminole Indian
    Reservation   49

Cable Beach   67
Cape Canaveral   4, 9, 32ff.
Cape Kennedy   32
Captiva   38, 40, **41f.**
Cat Island   84f.
Chub Cay   83
Clarence Town   85
Clearwater   38, **46f.**
Cockburn Town   86
Cocoa Beach   32
Conception Island   87
Congo Town   82
Crooked Island   87f.
Current Island   79
Cypress Gardens   4, 50

Daytona   13
Daytona Beach   34f.
Disney World, Walt   4, 8, 9,
    53ff.
Dunmore Town   79

Eglin Air Force Base   59
Elbow Cay   77
Eleuthera   79
Everglades National
    Park   5, 13, **19f.**
Exuma Cays   80ff.
Exuma Islands   80ff.

Family Islands   **77ff.**
Ferry   81
Florida City   13
Florida Keys   5, **13ff.**
Forbes Hill   81
Fort Lauderdale   4, 13,
    28ff.
Fort Myers   4, **40f.**
Fort Myers Beach   40f.
Fort Walton Beach   59f.

Fortune Island   87
Freeport   62, **74ff.**

George Town   80
Governor's Harbour   79
Grand Bahama   62, 63,
    64, **74ff.**
Great Exuma   80
Great Guana Cay   77
Great Harbour Cay   83
Great Inagua   88
Green Turtle Cay   77
Gregory Town   79

Harbour Island   79
Hermitage   81
Holmes Beach   44
Homosassa Springs   47
Hope Town   77

Islamorada   16

Jacksonville   37
John Pennekamp Coral
    Reef State Park   13

Kennedy Space Center   9,
    32ff.
Key Biscayne   28
Key Colony Beach   16
Key Largo   14
Key West   5, 8, 13, **16ff.**
Kissimee   51

Lake Okeechobee   49
Lake Wales   50
Lake Windsor   88
Layton City   16
Little Exuma   80
Long Bay Cays   82
Long Island   85f.
Long Key   16
Longboat Key   44
Lucaya   62, **74ff.**

Man-O-War-Cay   78
Mangrove Cay   82
Marathon   16
Marco Island   38f.
Marsh Harbour   77
Matthew Town   88
Mayaguana   88
Melbourne   31
Melbourne Beach   31
Miami   4, 7, 13, **21ff.**
Miami Beach   4, **21ff.**
Morgan's Bluff   82

Naples   39f.
Nassau   62, 67, **68ff.**
New Plymouth   77
New Providence   62, 63,
    67ff.
Nicholl's Town   82

Ocala   57
Okeechobee   49
Orlando   4, 8, **51f.**
Ormond Beach   34

Palm Beach   13, **30f.**
Panama City   59
Panama City Beach   59
Paradise Island   67, **71**
Pensacola   9, **60**
Pine Island   40
Port Howe   85
Punta Gorda   9

Red Bay Village   82
Redington   44
Rock Sound   79, 80
Rolle Town   81
Rolleville   81
Rum Cay   86f.

San Salvador   64, **86f.**
Sanibel   40, **41f.**
Sarasota   42f.
Sea World   52f.
Sebring   50
Spanish Wells   79
St Petersburg   8, 38, **44ff.**
St Petersburg Beach   44
Staniard Creek   82
Staniel Cay   80
Stella Maris   85
Steventon   81
Stocking Island   81

Tallahassee   6, 9, **59**
Tampa   47f.
Treasure Cay   77
Treasure Island   44

Upper Matecumbe   16

Vaca Key   16
Venice   43

Walker's Cay   77ff.
Weeki Wachee   47
West Palm Beach   4, 30
William's Town   81
Winter Haven   51

Original German text: Peter and Heinz Göckeritz. Translation: Barbara Cresswell
Series editor, English edition: Jane Rolph

© Verlag Robert Pfützner GmbH, München. Original German edition

© Jarrold Publishing, Norwich, Great Britain 1/91. English language edition worldwide

Published in the US and Canada by Hunter Publishing, Inc.,
300 Raritan Center Parkway, Edison NJ 08818

Illustrations: J. Allan Cash Ltd. pages 25, 86; J. Davis Travel Photography Ltd. pages 58, 69, 81, 82;
L. Ferguson pages 52 (top left), 54 (bottom); R. Gant pages 32 (right), 45 (top), 52 (top right); A. Hawkins pages 3,
14 (top), 24, 29, 39, 40, 44, 45 (bottom), 46, 47, 48 (bottom), 50 (top), 52 (bottom), 54 (top), 57 (both);
R. Howard pages 31, 32 (left); A. Roberts pages 5, 10; USTTA (Audience Planners) pages 41, 59, 60;
F. Weston page 92; D. White pages 1, 56; World Pictures Ltd. pages 13, 14 (bottom), 22, 34, 36, 61, 71, 75; ©
Walt Disney Company 1991 pages 7, 53 (both).

Printed in Italy

ISBN 0–7117–0482–1